Connecting Kids

Exploring Diversity together

Connecting Kids

Exploring Diversity together

Linda D. Hill

Foreword by Rick Scott

NEW SOCIETY PUBLISHERS

Canadian Cataloging in Publication Data

Hill, Linda, 1954-

Connecting Kids

Includes bibliographical references and index
ISBN 0-86571-431-2

1. Discrimination – Prevention – Study and teaching – Activity Programs
2. Prejudices in children – Prevention – Study and teaching – Activity Programs
i. Title
BF723.P75H54 2000   305'.083   C99-910733-X

Book and cover design by Kim Barnard of Graphic Details,
    inspired by the fun fonts and animal critters from Ethan Dunham of Fonthead Design
Cartoons of kids at play by Robert McKenzie Graphic Design Services
Cover paintings and community recreation illustrations by Ian Finlayson Illustration and Design

Printed in Canada on acid-free, partially recycled (20 percent post-consumer) paper using soy-based inks by Transcontinental/Best Book Manufacturers.

Inquiries regarding requests to reprint all or part of *Connecting Kids: Exploring Diversity Together* should be addressed to New Society Publishers at the address below.

To order directly from either publisher, please add $4.00 shipping to the price of the first copy, and $1.00 for each additional copy (plus GST in Canada).

Co-published by

New Society Publishers, P.O. Box 189, Gabriola Island, BC, V0R 1X0, Canada

New Society Publishers aims to publish books for fundamental social change through nonviolent action. We focus especially on sustainable living, progressive leadership, and educational and parenting resources. Our full list of books can be browsed on the worldwide web at: www.newsociety.com

in association with

Building Bridges Consulting, P.O. Box 156, Duncan, BC, V9L 3X3, Canada

We bring people together to share our rights and responsibilities to care for each other and for the Earth. Visit our website at www.island.net/~bridges/

NEW SOCIETY PUBLISHERS
www.newsociety.com

Building Bridges Consulting
www.island.net/~bridges/

Dedication

To Aunty Bette and all pioneers who
helped the children of the twentieth century
begin to explore diversity.

Table of Contents

My Family

O-oh, now what do you see
look out world it's my family
oh, now what can it be
look out world it's my family

I've got sisters
brothers and mothers
fathers, uncles and aunts
I've got relatives, I've got enemies
they'd be my friend if they'd give me a chance

There are black ones
white ones and red ones
brown ones and yellow ones too
so many colours are in my family
I wonder if any of them are blue

There are Taoists, Buddhists, Hindus
Christians, Muslims and Jews
I know someone who doesn't believe anything
I saw them once on the six o'clock news

O-oh, now what do you see
look out world it's my family
oh, now what can it be
look out world it's my family

LYRICS TO "MY FAMILY" BY RICK SCOTT,
FROM HIS ALBUM *RICK AROUND THE ROCK* ©1992 GRAND POOBAH MUSIC.
REPRINTED HERE WITH PERMISSION.

Foreword

Funny, isn't it? In this "age of communication" people are having so much difficulty communicating with each other. It's becoming harder and harder for us to express our feelings and be heard. Fear, anger, prejudice and bullying seem to be everywhere.

This situation appears so complicated, but perhaps a solution can be as simple as a child's game or a belly laugh. I am a great believer in the power of fun.

People don't seem to think fun applies to serious things. Too often it is held out as a reward for getting through a crummy time. But fun is powerful medicine which needs to be pushed to the front of the line, before diagnoses, therapies, exercises, judgments and resolutions.

Making music with children I am constantly reminded that laughter is an international language. A little bit of fun goes a long way to bridge gaps of age, language, race, class and gender.

Before we replace the sense of wonder with the load of logic, let us show and teach the power of community through the strength of song and the safety of games.

Linda's book re-introduces fun as a prac-*tickle* resource for resolving and celebrating our differences. Here is a manual for the funster in us all!

Here is a manual for the funster in us all!

Rick Scott
Philharmonic Fool

"Isn't it splendid to think of all the things there are to find out about?
It just makes me feel glad to be alive — it's such an interesting world.
It wouldn't be half so interesting if we knew all about everything,
would it? There'd be no scope for imagination then, would there?"

ANNE SHIRLEY
— FROM L. M. MONTGOMERY (1908) **ANNE OF GREEN GABLES**

How To Use This Book

Connecting Kids is designed from beginning to end to be an educational, inspirational, practical and fun guidebook. Information presented on the right hand pages is illustrated on the left hand pages by a scrapbook collection of stories and creative memorabilia that have enriched my own voyages of discovery over the years.

This back and forth balancing act of prose and poetry sets the stage for the main purpose of *Connecting Kids* which is to show how to guide children from different backgrounds to include each other in an atmosphere of safety, equality, choice and fun. All of the cooperative games, creative activities and nature experiences are organized according to twenty connecting skills that are especially important for learning to be welcoming and welcomed.

Follow these simple steps whenever you are looking for an activity idea:

1. Turn the page to the connecting skill you want to pass on to the children you are guiding and read through the definition and illustrations.

2. Look through the assortment of cooperative games, creative activities, and nature experiences that provide opportunities to practice this connecting skill.

3. Choose, adapt, combine or invent one or more games or activities that will engage you and the children in developing that connecting skill as you explore diversity.

4. Now gather the kids together and have fun on your journeys into your increasingly diverse communities!

As you play, appreciate all of the people who have participated in inventing, reinventing and sharing so many wonderful games, activities and experiences. Like the recipes for cooking, the recipes for play are not copyrighted. They are freely passed around the world in a never-ending relay of joy, love and laughter.

Para los niños trabajamos,

We work for children,

porque los niños son los que saben querer,

because children are the ones who know what is needed,

porque los niños son la esperanza del mundo.

because children are the hope of the world.

FROM JOSÉ MARTI (1889) **LA EDAD DE ORO** (THE GOLDEN AGE)

Part 1:

Making A Difference Together

If Wishes Could Make A Difference

When I wish upon a star I wish…

other kids could understand that I have feelings too

I could learn not to be so shy so that I could make some friends

my kids could get to know children with disabilities and all sorts of other differences

my child could be part of a friendly group of kids who care

children will value who they are instead of always trying to conform

kids could stop fighting and get along better

I could stand up for my friends

children could get over their fears of differences

When I wish upon a star, I want to stop…
- being used
- being out on the street
- being bullied or babied
- and I want to stop kids being picked on

When I wish upon a star, I think about the disappointment on my son's face when his siblings are out playing with friends and he's at home alone.

When I wish upon a star I think: *"Some kids may not be the same as you or they may not have as many friends but you don't need to tease them."*

My dream, when I wish upon a star, is to be able to bring all our differences together and realize that we can make some really beautiful things happen that we couldn't otherwise do.

Inclusive Travel Guides Needed Now

Children growing up during the beginning of this brand new millennium are living in the first generation in the history of the world when exploring our differences has become part of everyday life. Children of all ages, and from all sorts of cultures, countries, languages, heritages, religions, abilities, economic circumstances, lifestyles and other backgrounds are meeting each other in the places we live, learn, work, play and worship. Opportunities for adventures as life-changing as travelling to different countries around the world are now close at hand, just around the corner in every community.

Children need guidance to learn how to travel outside their familiar circles to get to know others from different backgrounds. Skilled and experienced explorers can help children discover new viewpoints showing how differences enrich our communities. Inclusive travel guides are needed everywhere in our increasingly diverse world:

> *Children need guidance to learn how to travel outside their familiar circles to get to know others from different backgrounds.*

- ◎ at home and in the neighborhood

- ◎ schools, community centers, drop-in programs and after-school day care centers

- ◎ camps, recreation programs and outdoor education centers

- ◎ sports teams, children's clubs and youth groups

- ◎ churches, temples and other places where we worship

- ◎ health centers, hospitals, group homes and other places children go for help and kind treatment

Everyone who is good with children and interested in people's differences has the potential to become an inclusive travel guide. Inclusive travel guides could be:

- ◎ relatives, friends and neighbors

- ◎ leaders of children's groups, coaches of sports teams and camp counsellors

- ◎ early childhood educators, day care supervisors and baby-sitters

- ◎ teachers, teaching assistants, playground supervisors, peer counsellors and other people who help children at school

- ◎ child and youth care workers, support workers, counsellors, therapists and other people who help children who are going through difficult times

- ◎ ecologists, biologists, zoologists, naturalists and everyone who loves nature

- ◎ writers, story tellers, singers, magicians, dulcimer players and other entertainers

- ◎ people of all cultures, ages, abilities and life-styles who live in cities, towns, villages, farms, camps, cabins and any other kind of community

Imagine what an enjoyable voyage of discovery life can become when children feel safe enough to share their unique gifts, to choose how to be and to communicate together through the universal language of fun!

ABOUT SEGREGATION

Left to their own devices, children deal with differences by dividing themselves up into separate social realms. Graduates from the same high school were quickly able to make a map of their school showing where the "Jocks", "Shrubs", "Preppies", "Sikhs", "First Nations", and "Nerds" hung out. Within these circles of like-minded peers, everyone can use the same language, behave in similar ways, dress alike, share the same values, and follow the leaders who decide who can do what and who can hang around with whom. Outsiders are identified and labelled so that they may be more easily avoided. Disputes over differences can escalate from name-calling to physical fighting. Children who are different in ways that don't fit into any group are rejected as "weird", "hyper", "retarded", or "gross". Left alone, these kids are vulnerable to teasing and bullying from all sides.

by Danika Carlson, age 6

by Jana Vance, age 13

by Sylvie Emouts, age 9

About Segregation

Some people deal with differences by staying apart and only associating with people who are the same. Avoiding and excluding differences is called **segregation**. Sorting children into schools, camps, teams or cliques according to their skin color, type of disability, wealth, age or talents are examples of segregation. Up until the 1970s, segregation was the most common way of dealing with differences.

Inclusive travel guides can help transform any group into a more considerate and more closely knit team.

The main advantages of dividing up into groups of similar people are comfort, efficiency and productivity. Team work goes smoothly when everyone talks the same language, follows the same rules and goes at the same pace. Cultural and national identities flourish in segregated settings. Segregation allows individuals to get together to develop highly specialized interests and talents. Dividing up into separate teams of equal ability promotes fiercely exciting competition.

A big disadvantage of segregation is that it is often unfair. One kind of unfairness is when someone is not allowed to be part of a group they would like to belong to. Another kind of unfairness is when members of one or more groups have more resources or take control of members of the smaller groups. Members of an entire group can be left out or treated badly by the members of other groups. Members of different groups may dislike each other and be afraid of each other. Racism, sexism, able-ism, elitism and other forms of prejudice divide and conquer people.

In segregated settings, inclusive travel guides can help transform any group into a more considerate and more closely knit team who are more aware of each other's differences as gifts. Bringing separate groups of children together to explore their differences is even more exciting. Meeting together in an atmosphere of safety, equality, choice and fun is a highly effective means of breaking down walls of prejudice and discrimination.

ABOUT INTEGRATION

Children need guidance to learn how differences can enrich a group. No one at summer camp could remember why they had all rejected Ken. One of his cabin mates recalled that he had played with Ken on the first day. *"Then the next day everyone just told me to stop playing with him, so I did."* Fortunately, a camp counsellor who had inclusive leadership skills noticed that Ken was being left out. He took the time to guide Ken and the other boys in his cabin to get to know each other, include each other and look out for each other. Released from fears of being put down or being pushed out, the boys relaxed and opened up to each other's unique personalities. They incorporated Ken's interests in artificial intelligence into a science fiction play that they performed on the last night of camp. Ken's farewell card to his camp counsellor said, *"This was the best summer of my life. I made some friends out of it who like me the way I am."*

by Jana Vance, age 13

Too often, children are socially isolated in the midst of integrated settings. Don grew up Deaf in a Hearing community. At school he was provided with the interpreting and tutoring supports he needed to fit in academically, but he was very unhappy socially. *"Ninety percent of the kids in the school didn't know me and didn't want to know me. Five percent of the kids in my school knew me and hated me. There were five percent who would play with me but I hated them."* By the time he was a teenager, Don also hated most things about himself and about being Deaf. He spent hours watching the same teenage horror videos over and over, fantasizing ways of getting revenge against the students who bullied him and the others who had stood by and done nothing to help him. *"They treated me like I was an outsider. It was insulting when kids wouldn't play with me, or called me names. But it was even worse when they planned parties right in front of me as if I were invisible. Sometimes I would do things on purpose to provoke a fight because the physical pain was preferable to the emotional blocks. That feeling of being less than nothing has made me into a lonely person and put a stop to things like trying to set goals."* Even today after changing schools, seeing counsellors and experiencing many practical successes such as meeting other Deaf students, finding a part time job, getting a driver's license and buying a car, Don continues to describe himself as a loner. *"I guess I've let all this stuff that I've gone through get me down to the point that I don't trust too many people."*

About Integration

Some people deal with differences by helping everyone join the same group. Inviting people from smaller groups into the larger group is called **integration**. Human rights movements during the 1960s, '70s and '80s increased integration throughout many communities. Mainstreaming students from segregated schools and special classes into regular classrooms in local schools is an example of integration.

When children become more accommodating, accepting and supportive of each other's different backgrounds, self-esteem builds and there is less isolation.

Integration has three main advantages. First, everyone has opportunities to participate in what the bigger group is doing. Second, pooling everyone's resources gives the entire group a competitive advantage in getting things accomplished. Third, learning to work and play together as equals instead of separately can dissolve the problems of prejudice and nurture the seeds of friendship.

A major disadvantage of integration is that people's individual, social, cultural and spiritual identities may be submerged. Joining the mainstream means living in the midst of pressures to leave one's differences behind and conform to the ways of the majority. People who do not want to or are not able to be like everyone else struggle against the flow or get swept to the edges of the current.

Inclusive travel guides can guide children in any integrated setting to find the wider places in the mainstream where the current slows down and the waters are deeper and calmer. When children become more accommodating, accepting and supportive of each other's different backgrounds, self-esteem builds and there is less isolation. With guidance, children can find their identities within an integrated setting and find peaceful resolutions to misunderstandings and conflicts related to their differences.

ABOUT INTERACTION

"We come together in dignity,
bringing our gifts to share
Finding places we've never been
and bringing our new friends there."

COLLABORATIVE POEM BY SUSAN, DONALD, ESTELLA AND SHERRY, 1996
FROM LINDA HILL (1998) **DISCOVERING CONNECTIONS**. DUNCAN:
BUILDING BRIDGES. REPRINTED HERE WITH PERMISSION.

by Jana Vance, age 13

Our rights:

✔ To be safe
✔ To belong
✔ To share our many gifts
✔ To ask for help
✔ To be respected

Our responsibilities:

✔ To keep safe
✔ To welcome
✔ To accept our many gifts
✔ To offer to help
✔ To be respectful

About Interaction

Some people deal with differences by building bridges across differences. Getting together to exchange different knowledge, ideas and points of view is called **interaction**. Student exchange programs, multi-cultural community celebrations, mixed-income housing and cooperative learning communities are examples of interaction. The dawn of this new millennium is a time of discovering more and more opportunities for people from different backgrounds to learn from each other by interacting together.

People become more understanding of each other and more patient when differences are viewed as gifts to exchange instead of problems to be eliminated.

The main advantages of interaction are dramatic improvements in how people get along. People become more understanding of each other and more patient when differences are viewed as gifts to exchange instead of problems to be eliminated. Increasing communication and cooperation are both highly effective in reducing bullying, intolerance, rejection and conflict.

Two main disadvantages of interaction are that taking the time to build bridges across differences slows things down and interactive groups lose their competitive edge. When relationships with each other become more important than the final destination, people are not as oriented to getting things accomplished. Spending extra time together feels wonderful in an atmosphere of laughter, joy and celebration but frustrations can build when it becomes hard to figure out how to get work done.

In an interactive group where differences are already being embraced and celebrated, inclusive travel guides can lead children to explore the tensions between work and play as another interesting difference to explore. Inclusive travel guides can also sensitize children to new kinds of differences and can guide children to take actions that transform inclusive dreams, experiments and explorations into on-going personal, group and community-wide changes.

LEARNING
CONNECTING
SKILLS

by Harvey Jimmy, age 18

We always began our group by contributing our thoughts and feelings to the **Talking Circle** (page 89). I thought I understood that in a Talking Circle the person holding the feather is the only one who talks, so it really irritated me when Kelly kept interrupting and adding her two cents in at the end of what each person said. *"We need to take her aside and tell her to stop doing that!"* I suggested to Colleen, my co-leader. *"There is no need to take her aside. She will learn best by watching us listen,"* Colleen replied patiently. So, somewhat grudgingly, I gave up my plan of taking Kelly aside to give her a lecture on respect. (Come to think of it, she had probably had at least 9,999 lectures from adults on that topic in her brief thirteen years of life experience so far). Instead, I began focusing on what Colleen was doing that was helping her to be so much calmer, patient and understanding than I seemed to be able to be. Watching my wise co-facilitator carefully, I observed that as each child held the feather and spoke, Colleen listened so attentively and completely, that — for Colleen — there were no distractions and no interruptions. Nothing else was in that moment except for her unconditionally loving relationship with the child holding the feather. The more I watched, the more I was able to imitate Colleen's style of listening. Gradually, I became more and more able to focus completely on the heart to heart communication coming from the child holding the feather. The distraction I had been creating for myself through my irritation with Kelly dissolved. By watching and listening, instead of reacting and responding, Kelly and I learned together how to tune in and understand what each person had to teach us.

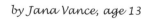

by Jana Vance, age 13

Learning Connecting Skills

Inclusive travel guides are continually developing our own skills for welcoming children and adults of all ages, abilities and backgrounds to connect together in ways that are safe, equal, respectful and fun. At the same time, we are continually passing these skills for connecting on to the children and adults we are guiding. The more everyone shares in learning and practicing the skills for connecting across differences, the more everyone can realize their rights and responsibilities to include and to be included.

We learn by watching and listening to other people who know how to connect with others, by practicing with others and by getting feedback about how we are doing.

Children and adults of all ages, abilities and backgrounds can learn social skills for connecting with others just as easily as learning to do a chore, read a book, play a musical instrument, swim across a pool, paint a picture or build a double-decker bridge-fort. We learn by watching and listening to other people who know how to connect with others, by practicing with others and by getting feedback about how we are doing.

There are hundreds and hundreds of skills for connecting across differences. Some connecting skills are as easy as joining a circle. Other connecting skills are as complex as learning a new language. *Connecting Kids* defines and describes twenty connecting skills that seem to be especially important for exploring diversity. My first book, *Discovering Connections,* contains twenty more connecting skills. Also see pages 158–159 for a few more books about social skills.

Connecting skills for inclusive travel guides...

  1 **JOINING THE CIRCLE** involves gathering in a group, welcoming each other, following directions and paying attention to each other in order to do things together.

  2 **MODELING** is whatever we are doing while people who admire us and want to be like us are watching. We teach and learn almost everything by modeling and copying.

  **3** **BREAKING THE ICE** means warming the atmosphere in ways that release tension, energize the group, build trust and open up everyone's creativity.

  4 **PARTICIPATORY PACING** is when you set an active pace while making smooth transitions and individual adjustments to keep everyone involved. Paying close attention to feedback from participants is the key.

  5 **I'LL BE YOUR PARTNER!** involves doing things with different people instead of always sticking with the same partner. All games and activities can be adapted in ways that children can play in partners or small groups.

  **6** **GIVE AND TAKE** means offering a contribution, accepting what is being offered back and then offering another contribution. Playing catch or having a conversation are both examples of give and take.

  7 **TOUCH CONTROL AND OTHER SAFETY SKILLS** are acquired through respecting each other's physical boundaries, even in crowded places and even when playing fast-paced games.

  8 **DARING TO BE DIFFERENT** means building pride in each other's unique gifts, talents, special qualities, cultural backgrounds, lifestyles, abilities and disabilities that make the world a more interesting place.

  9 **FOLLOWING THE LEADERS BEHIND YOU** involves seeking out contributions from the people on the outskirts. The leaders in the back of a group can see things from different angles and they can view things in completely new ways.

  10 **UNDERSTANDING IN ANY LANGUAGE** is acquiring the ability to listen carefully with your heart, eyes and ears to many different kinds of communication. Relax, repeat back what you understand and accept support from interpreters when needed.

...to develop and pass on to others!

For the BIG picture, turn to:

TUNING IN means putting yourself into another person's place by joining your ears, eyes and hearts in harmony with the other person's feelings, ideas and experiences. When children are in tune, they can all be heard.

 page 85

BRINGING IN THE REINFORCEMENTS means strengthening each other's abilities and confidence by getting involved in activities and interactions that immediately lead to enjoyable results and positive feedback.

 page 91

GIVING A HAND is offering to help in ways that guide others to safety or to more choice, more power and more fun. Sharing, doing something for someone, hand-over-hand guidance, showing and comforting are all ways of giving a hand.

 page 97

OFF-STAGE PROMPTING is when you give cues through words, pictures or actions that help others figure out what to do or say next. Prompting without coming across as nagging is a real balancing act.

 page 103

LEAVING OUT LOSING involves adapting games and activities so that no one gets left out or eliminated. Everyone has more fun when children play with each other instead of against each other.

 page 109

KEEPING COOL WHEN THINGS GET HOT means staying calm and remembering to encourage others even when you are under pressure. Children can learn to keep cool by participating in activities that are difficult but not impossible.

 page 115

PRACTICING TOLERANCE involves steadfastly ignoring something that bothers you while simultaneously searching for positive aspects of the person or the situation to support and strengthen.

 page 121

NO-GO-TELL means standing up for safety by saying "No" to dangerous or potentially dangerous situations, going away, helping others to get away and telling someone who can help you.

 page 127

CHALLENGE BY CHOICE means taking realistic risks within a safety net of trust, mutual caring and confidence. Daring to stretch and try leads to growth and turns life into an exciting adventure.

 page 133

INVENTING NEW POSSIBILITIES involves solving problems and overcoming barriers by sharing ideas, trying experiments and coming up with new ways of doing things.

 page 139

The most inclusive things in life are free!

One of the main ways to bridge economic differences is to explore free and inexpensive games, activities and experiences.

Play with equipment that is easy to find:

- *balls of all shapes, weights and sizes*
- *rope, hoops, wheels, sticks, nets, skipping ropes*
- *blocks, building sets, anything that stacks*
- *paper, scissors, hammers, saws*
- *playing cards, dice, board games*
- *dress up clothes, hats, costumes, masks, dolls, puppets, stuffed animals*
- *pipes, drums, strings, other musical instruments*
- *cardboard boxes, sheets, blankets*
- *boundaries and playing areas drawn with chalk, marked out with rope or marked out by the features of the area*
- *the natural environment including forests, rivers, rocks, fields, beaches, mountains*

Create with free and inexpensive materials:

- *seeds, macaroni, cereal, flour, water, oil, food coloring, sugar, fruit, vegetables, eggs*
- *sand, pebbles, wood, nails, screws*
- *drawings, photographs, old magazines, old newspapers*
- *face cream, make-up, soap*
- *paint, chalk, crayons, felt markers, pencils, glue*
- *paper plates, string, straws, tin cans, corks, balloons*
- *buttons, old socks, scraps of cloth, wool*
- *roll-ends of newsprint available from newspaper publishers and moving companies*

Explore these community resources:

- *a gym or playground and all the equipment for physical adventures*
- *a dance studio or a stage with lighting and sound systems*
- *a kitchen with an oven, stove, blender, kettle, freezer, pots, pans, other cooking utensils*
- *a gardening shed with shovels, hoes, wheel barrows, buckets*
- *a workshop with saws, hammers, drills, nails, screws*
- *a meeting room with tables, chairs, overhead projector*
- *a museum or nature center with displays, microscopes, telescopes*
- *libraries and resource centers with CDs, tapes, old-fashioned records, videos, books, video camera, video tape machine, editing equipment*
- *shopping plazas, malls, downtown shopping areas*
- *plays, shows and other entertaining events in the community*
- *parks and camps with trails, fields, beaches, picnic areas*
- *elders, entertainers, artists, teachers, nature interpreters, visitors and others who are willing to pass their different learnings on to children*

Learning through play

Cooperative games, creative arts and nature contain endless opportunities for children to learn connecting skills as they play. Children learn as they chase, hide, do tricks, race, climb, lift and carry, tell stories, ask questions, guess, act, draw, paint, write, decipher codes and signals, make music, observe plants and animals, solve problems, invent, dance, build, do experiments and experience so many other ways of playing.

Our complicated world becomes simpler and learning feels fun and easy when we play cooperatively, create and experience nature together. Rules are clear. Challenges are possible. Patterns are beautiful. A few new skills are learned at a time. Each skill is practiced over and over again and there are always interesting surprises and developments to keep everyone's interest. Playing, creating and exploring are easy when everyone shares in figuring out so many different ways that children of different ages, abilities, incomes, interests and other backgrounds can take part.

With practice, inclusive leaders can pass on skills through play as easily as preparing a meal or singing a song. The connecting skills are the basic ingredients and musical beat. Keeping those skills in mind, flip through *Connecting Kids* and other books and brainstorm with others. Try out something new, think of one of your old favorites or experiment with putting several ideas together into new combinations. In the same way that creative cooks prepare delicious meals or musicians compose new music, use your imagination to mix and match ideas, equipment, actions and activities to produce endless varieties of fun things to do that fit with any occasion or anyone's differences. Homemade food tastes better, homemade music sounds better and homemade activities feel better; especially when everyone has contributed their potluck ideas and unique talents. Inclusive groups NEVER have too many cooks to spoil the broth or too many instruments to beat the band. The most delicious feasts or creative jam sessions of all are when everyone has become so involved that it is impossible to find the chief cook and bottle washer or figure out just who the composer was.

Use your imagination to mix and match ideas, equipment, actions and activities to produce endless varieties of fun things to do that fit with any occasion or anyone's differences.

Tip: As the children you are guiding become aware of the connecting skills they are learning, they will come up with endless ideas for more adventures that will give opportunities to practice those skills.

My Friend
Has The Biggest Ears
In The World

My friend, my friend
has the biggest ears in the world
till North is South and East is West
my friend and his ears are the best

They are so huge, well one day we were playing
we got hit by a terrible storm
so we wrapped his ears around us with room to spare
we were laughing, we were dry, we were warm

They are so awesome, well they flap in the wind
we're afraid he might blow away
but he makes them like wings and we all climb on board
fly away to our own holiday

'cause he's my friend, he's my best buddy
and he has the biggest ears in the world
till North is South and East is West
my friend and his ears are the best

LYRICS TO "MY FRIEND HAS THE BIGGEST EARS IN THE WORLD" BY RICK AND JORG SCOTT, FROM *THE ELECTRIC SNOWSHOE* ©1989 GRAND POOBAH MUSIC. REPRINTED HERE WITH PERMISSION.

Part 2:

Let's Go Exploring!

JOINING THE CIRCLE

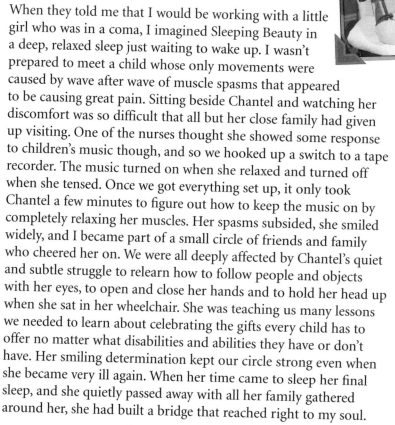

When they told me that I would be working with a little girl who was in a coma, I imagined Sleeping Beauty in a deep, relaxed sleep just waiting to wake up. I wasn't prepared to meet a child whose only movements were caused by wave after wave of muscle spasms that appeared to be causing great pain. Sitting beside Chantel and watching her discomfort was so difficult that all but her close family had given up visiting. One of the nurses thought she showed some response to children's music though, and so we hooked up a switch to a tape recorder. The music turned on when she relaxed and turned off when she tensed. Once we got everything set up, it only took Chantel a few minutes to figure out how to keep the music on by completely relaxing her muscles. Her spasms subsided, she smiled widely, and I became part of a small circle of friends and family who cheered her on. We were all deeply affected by Chantel's quiet and subtle struggle to relearn how to follow people and objects with her eyes, to open and close her hands and to hold her head up when she sat in her wheelchair. She was teaching us many lessons we needed to learn about celebrating the gifts every child has to offer no matter what disabilities and abilities they have or don't have. Her smiling determination kept our circle strong even when she became very ill again. When her time came to sleep her final sleep, and she quietly passed away with all her family gathered around her, she had built a bridge that reached right to my soul.

E pe bo mi, omo
Gather round me children, Gather round me

Gege b'irawo
Like stars around the moon

Ti pe b'osupa e pe
Gather round me.

(NIGERIAN LULLABY)

by Rachel and Nathan Singleton-Polster, ages 9 & 11

SKILL 1: JOINING THE CIRCLE

Circles are the foundation of team work and are the essence of community building. A circle symbolizes unity in many languages. In American Sign Language, the sign for cooperation is formed by linking two circles together and moving them in one big circle.

As children learn to join in a circle they are learning to:

- pay attention to each other
- do things in unison
- stay with the group
- follow directions

Inclusive leaders can stand beside children who are just learning circle skills to more easily show what to do, to give a hand if needed and to supervise children who need to take a break. Inclusive leaders review and demonstrate the inclusive ground rules of safety, equality, choice and fun for those children who are just beginning to explore diversity.

Exploring diversity involves keeping our circles open and stretching our arms wide enough to welcome everyone who arrives. Whenever I feel like giving up on someone who is really difficult to include in a circle, I remind myself to be persistently welcoming. I try to creatively find ways to guide children from the disconnected places they are used to being, toward the unfamiliar joy of participating with a supportive, cooperative group.

Stand beside children who are just learning circle skills to more easily show what to do.

Tip: Children who are used to excluding others from their circles will become more and more welcoming if they have inclusive guidance from leaders who they admire and look up to. It takes time, practice and encouragment for connecting skills to become automatic.

the possibilities
for games and
activities that
use blankets and
parachutes are as
endless as a circle.

Here are cooperative games and activities that give children enjoyable opportunities to participate in circles where everyone is welcome to join in.

Blankets And Parachutes

Holding on to a blanket or a parachute is a wonderful way for children to learn to gather into a circle.

◎ Lift it up high and smile at each other. Take turns hiding under it or running under it. Shake your blanket to make waves and other patterns.

◎ Hold on tight for blanket aerobics and blanket dances. Try walking, skipping, jumping to the right, to the left and in one place.

◎ Play ball! Bounce a soft ball up and down. Watch how high and count how many times you can bounce it. Then try rolling the ball around and around or sending it back and forth from one person to another. If you have a parachute that has a hole in the middle, see if you can get a hole-in-one. See if you can make the ball travel through waves. Add more soft balls of different sizes.

◎ Take turns going underneath the blanket and try to bounce the balls out as they bounce or roll around.

◎ Put a bunch of soft nerf balls, beach balls and balloons on the blanket and wait for someone to call out "Popcorn!", then pop all of the balls out of the blanket.

◎ Get into circles around two blankets and bounce a ball back and forth from one blanket to the other.

◎ Tell stories while everyone uses the blanket to show the actions. Wave the blanket to show wind or waves. Drum on the blanket to show footsteps across hard ground or raindrops falling from the sky. Rub the blanket to show going through tall grass. Put a hand under the blanket to show a many legged worm, an elephant or a bubble of gas rising out of the swamp.

The possibilities for games and activities that use blankets and parachutes are as endless as a circle.

Hot Potato

One child goes in the middle and waits while everyone passes a potato as quickly as possible around the circle. A sock, hat, bean bag or ball are all fine substitutes for a potato. Children often enjoy chanting a counting rhyme while the potato goes around such as:

"One potato, two potato, three potato, four! Five potato, six potato, seven potato, more!"

When the potato gets so hot that it drops, everyone yells "Too hot to handle!" The child in the middle picks the potato up, trades places with the child who dropped it, and the game starts all over again. When you are playing this game with a large circle of children, add more potatoes and send more children into the middle.

Duck, Duck, Goose Name Game

In this variation on **Duck, Duck, Goose** everyone stands in a circle and one child goes around the outside, stopping briefly behind each person, getting their attention and saying their name followed by the word "duck". For example: "Tristan duck", "Petra duck", "Ramen duck", "Jenean duck", "Nonie duck" and so on.

There are many ways of getting each person's attention, such as tapping each person lightly on the shoulder, shaking hands held behind backs and/or getting visual contact. Everyone helps with the challenge of understanding and remembering names. At some point, instead of saying "Duck" after a person's name, the child says "Goose!" For example: "Brenda Goose!" This is the signal for both children to race around the circle in opposite directions back to Brenda's spot. Brenda now has a turn to go around the circle naming each person and saying "duck" after each name until… she says a name and then "Goose!" and races around the circle again.

Who, Who

This is a great way of welcoming new children into a circle. Imagine that you have two new children in a group named Melba and Carson. Introduce Melba to the first person on your right:

Leader: "This is Melba."
Right 1: "Who?"
Leader: "This is Melba."
Right 1: "Oh, Melba! Nice to meet you." Now Right 1 turns to the person on her right and introduces Melba.

Right 1: "This is Melba."
Right 2: "Who?"
Right 1: (Turns to Leader) "Who?"
Leader: "This is Melba."
Right 1: (Turns to Right 2) "This is Melba."
Right 2: "Oh, Melba! Nice to meet you." Right 2 turns to the person on his right and introduces Melba.

Everyone helps with the challenge of understanding and remembering names.

Right 2: "This is Melba."
Right 3: "Who?"
Right 2: (Turns to Right 1) "Who?"
Right 1: (Turns to Leader) "Who?"
Leader: "This is Melba."
Right 1: (Turns to Right 2) "This is Melba."
Right 2: (Turns to Right 3) "This is Melba."
Right 3: "Oh, Melba! Nice to meet you." Right 3 turns to the person on his right and introduces Melba. And so on…

As Melba gets introduced around the circle, this "Who, Who?" sequence gets longer and longer because the question goes all the way back to the leader each time before it gets answered.

Once everyone is familiar with the pattern, but just before the game gets boring, you begin to introduce Carson around the circle, beginning with the person on the left. Now that the "Who, who" sequence is going around the circle both ways, things get

(continued on the next page)

JOINING
THE
CIRCLE

(Who, Who continued)

a little more complicated but are manageable so long as you, the leader, stay on your toes and keep the names straight as you answer the "Who, Who" questions coming at you from left as well as right. The game often becomes completely impossible with all the laughter going on at the point that the two children meet up during their introductory spin around the circle. Whether or not they manage to cross paths successfully, it is unlikely that anyone will forget the names of the people who got introduced during this circle game.

Add-on Tower Building

Each child takes a turn adding a block to build a tower in the middle of the circle. The tension builds around the circle as the tower goes higher and higher, it begins to wobble and parts fall off. The high point is when it all falls down! The motivation is to help each other build it even higher the next time. When I was a little kid, we used to spend an entire morning carefully constructing towers out of playing cards. One false move or a stray breeze and they would tumble down. Often we had as much fun building walled cities that stretched up and down the halls as we did building vertical structures. Other ideas for building materials are milk cartons, cardboard boxes or anything that will stack. You can even make a tower out of shoes. Here are some ideas for keeping everyone involved when there are more than about eight children in the group.

- ◎ Build towers in small groups and eventually link them together.
- ◎ Build one large tower with two children taking a turn each time.
- ◎ Build one tower by forming lines behind a central group of about four or six (like spokes in a wheel). After adding on to the tower, children go to the back of their spoke.

Folk Dancing

Sharing music and dance is one of the most popular ways for people from different backgrounds to relax together and learn from each other in a circle. Children enjoy building up a repertoire of favorites that they can sing and dance over and over.

- ◎ Beginning with simple words and movements, group members can take turns showing each other songs and dances.
- ◎ Invite people from a local dance group or a cultural society to come and teach you.
- ◎ Many children's entertainers and folk dancers have made videos and CDs that are easy to follow and learn from.

Magic Wand

In this mime activity, each child is encouraged to transform a 'magic wand' (a stick) into something different as it gets passed around the circle. One child might conduct an orchestra, another might turn that wand into a telescope, another might play a flute to charm a snake and so on. Try this activity again passing around a piece of newspaper, a ball, a scarf or almost any object. Try passing one object one way and another object the other way. The entire circle becomes magical when kids are encouraging each other to use their imaginations. Also see **Add-on Story Telling** (page 104).

the entire circle
becomes magical
when kids are
encouraging
each other
to use their
imaginations.

Making Butter

Pour whipping cream (the kind that comes in a carton, not the spray can kind) into a jar. Sit around a picnic blanket and take turns shaking the jar until the cream turns to butter. Then spread it on homemade bread or crackers. Delicious.

JOINING
THE
CIRCLE

Cooperative Drawing

Send creativity round and round the circle with this pass-it-on art activity. Sit on the floor or around a table and give each child a piece of paper and some crayons, felts, pastels, paints or other art supplies. Each child draws or colors for a short time, until it is time to pass the paper on (either to the right or the left). Each child continues drawing or coloring until it is time to pass the paper on again. Continue around the circle until each child has had a turn drawing or coloring on every piece of paper. Also see **Inclusive Assembly Line** (page 44) and **Cooperative Cards** (page 93).

- ◎ Children enjoy doing this activity while listening to a story or to music.

- ◎ Children can take turns adding to a sequence such as: Draw a head of any kind of person or animal (pass it on). Draw a neck (pass it on). Draw a body (pass it on). Draw a tail (pass it on). Draw legs (pass it on). Draw arms (pass it on). Draw feet (pass it on). Draw hands (pass it on).

Gathering Around Nature

Gather children in a circle again and again to learn about our most beautiful natural world.

- ◎ Gather around an ant hill, a wild life tree, a pond or a tide pool. When the season is right, gather in a circle to pick edible fruit.

- ◎ Stop anytime to take a closer look at a butterfly, a rock formation, a tadpole, a flower, a bird, a footprint or reflections of light playing with water.

- ◎ Lay down on your backs with your heads together and look up at the branches of trees, patterns of light and shadow, passing clouds, the rain coming down or the night sky.

- ◎ Sit back to back in a still and close circle and wait for nature to gather around you.

Gather children in a circle again and again to learn about our most beautiful natural world.

Around The Campfire

Singing songs and telling stories while sitting around a campfire or a candle or even a flashlight is a wonderful way of gathering in a circle. To fill your circle with magical floating rainbows, hand out bubble wands and bubble mix and blow bubbles between stories and songs.

 Caution: Be sure to have plenty of adult supervision, and to follow all regulations and fire safety steps when having your campfire time.

MODELING

Getting involved in a summer culture camp gave Nicole opportunities to find new role models. *"I liked playing lots of fun games, starting to meet other people and learning our Indian language. Some people are out in the streets and they don't know nothing about their whole entire life. They don't even know their language. I don't want to be out on the street and I also noticed that I want to quit swearing and being rude. I get along with other people and play games now, I even get along with adults better than I used to because they have a lot of knowledge and wisdom to share in the stories about their life."*

"Haere mai ra" (Welcome—beckoning)   "Hoatu i taku ringa" (I offer you my hand)

"Ki ahau nei ra" (Come to me)   "Tahuri ke koe" (You turn your face away)

Maori Action Songs

Tessa, Tessa dressed in blue
Do these motions and we'll follow you.
Stand at attention, stand at ease
Bend your elbows, bend your knees
Point to red. Point to green.
Dive down deep in your yellow submarine
Touch sky, touch ground or stand on your head.
Now say good-bye and we'll follow Kara instead.

(CHILDREN'S SKIPPING SONG)

FROM ALAN ARMSTRONG (1986) **GAMES AND DANCES OF THE MAORI PEOPLE**. NEW ZEALAND: VIKING SEVENSEAS. REPRINTED WITH PERMISSION.

by Danika Carlson, age 6

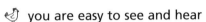 # SKILL 2: MODELING

MODELING

Modeling is a very powerful teaching tool in any culture. In fact, in many cooperative cultures around the world, it is considered very impolite to physically prompt or even to tell anyone — including children — what to do. Instead, children learn almost everything by watching. Children will copy you if:

- you are easy to see and hear
- you are doing something that is easy to imitate
- they admire you and want to be like you
- they see that you are doing something rewarding

The tricky part of modeling is that you cannot turn it on and off. Children model whatever leaders do, not just what they are told to do. If you want children to learn how to include each other then you need to make sure that all your interactions with other adults and children are welcoming and respectful. Children also copy other children, especially children who are popular, well liked and admired. With your guidance, these kids will learn to model inclusion and not exclusion.

Children model whatever leaders do, not just what they are told to do.

Tip: In any group, the more people there are who are well-liked, admired and who know how to interact safely, respectfully, equally and enjoyably; the easier it is to show others how to explore diversity in welcoming ways.

MODELING

Here are a few games and activities that give everyone opportunities to practice modeling and copying inclusive interactions. Everyone can learn to be a role model.

FOLLOW THE LEADER GAMES

There are probably hundreds of games in which different children take turns making actions for everyone to copy. Here are a few examples to get you started.

Everyone can learn to be a role model.

- **Follow the Leader Circle:** Leaders take turns coming into the center of the circle and making actions for everyone to follow. Then they spin around and select a new leader who hasn't had a turn yet.

- **Follow the Leader Parade:** Make a parade or a marching band and follow each other upstairs and downstairs. Go outdoors and follow the leader into the adventure playground, through fields, along trails or along a beach. When the lead child wants to, or gets tapped on the shoulder, the child behind takes over the lead and the past-leader goes to the back of the line.

- **Sit Down Follow the Leader:** Passing actions from one person to the next is a great way to make a long wait such as a bus ride go by very quickly.

- **Extrasensory Perception:** People take their turn being a leader as soon as they feel the right leadership 'vibes.'

- **Who is the Leader?:** In this game everyone stands in a circle and one or two children come into the center and hide their eyes. The rest of the group quietly select a leader to imitate. The leader tries to be as subtle as possible and the group tries to imitate as quickly as possible. When everyone is "in synch", the children in the middle open their eyes and guess who the leader is. If they guess wrong, the person who tricked them (by following the leader so closely that they seemed like the leader) comes in the middle to help. Now the children in the middle close their eyes again and wait for the group to pick a new leader and get "in synch" again. When they get the signal to open their eyes, they guess again. If they guess correctly, the leader comes into the middle of the circle and hides his or her eyes while everyone else goes back to the edge of the circle, selects another leader and gets "in synch" all over again.

- **Musical Follow the Leader:** First select a song everyone knows and get everyone to help you sing it, hum it or "La La La" the tune. Then select a leader to start "dancing" with one part of his or her body. The leader might try something a bit unusual like dancing an elbow, knee or shoulder. When everyone is copying the leader, a new leader begins to dance with another body part and everyone copies the new movement as well as doing the first movement. Another leader begins to dance with another body part and everyone adds in a third movement. Go for as long as you can, flowing from one creative dance to another. Some of the movements will drop off and others will continue. Sometimes groups discover the joy of following someone who makes an interesting accidental movement and an unexpected leader will emerge.

ECHO SONGS, POEMS AND STORIES

MODELING

In an echo song, the leader sings a phrase that is echoed by the rest of the group. This is a great way to learn a new song, so any song can be made into an echo song. However, the best echo songs are ones with lots of repetition or that develop a story sequence. In this song which can be sung to almost any tune, the echoing is in italics.

"There's a hole... *there's a hole...* there's a hole in the bottom of the sea."

"There's a log in the hole in the bottom of the sea... *there's a log in the hole in the bottom of the sea... (Chorus: There's a hole... there's a hole... there's a hole in the bottom of the sea).*"

"There's a bump on the log in the hole in the bottom of the sea... *(echo & chorus).*"

"There's a frog on the bump on the log in the hole in the bottom of the sea... *(echo & chorus).*"

"There's a wart on the frog on the bump on the log in the hole in the bottom of the sea... *(echo & chorus).*"

"There's a hair on the wart on the frog on the bump on the log in the hole in the bottom of the sea... *(echo & chorus).*"

"There's a fly on the hair on the wart on the frog on the bump on the log in the hole in the bottom of the sea... *(echo & chorus).*"

"There's a flea on the fly on the hair on the wart on the frog on the bump on the log in the hole in the bottom of the sea... *(echo & chorus).*"

Any song can be made into an echo song.

Children enjoy learning a few echo songs and singing them over and over. Invent and improvise echo songs, echo poems and echo stories by making up new sequences and new verses.

ACTION SONGS

Action songs have movements and gestures that go with the words. Sometimes they tell stories. Any song can be turned into an action song by an energetic and creative group, especially if someone in the group knows mime or sign language. Simply sing the song, add in the actions and get the group going. There are many ways to learn action songs.

- Trade action songs with each other.
- Watch children's entertainers and do their actions as you sing along.
- Go to the library and pick up books, videos and CDs filled with action songs.

STARS OF THE SILENT STAGE

Go to the library and borrow videos showing silent movies, clowns, mime performances and Theatre of the Deaf. Charlie Chaplin and Marcel Marceau will be easy to find. Perhaps you can find an old Mary Pickford movie or examples of Khon Theatre from Thailand, South Asian Folk Theatre or mime in India and Africa. Spend a rainy afternoon watching these videos and then make up your own silent performances. Imitation is the finest form of flattering these masters of movement. You might want to video tape your productions so that you can watch them on another rainy day.

MODELING

MODELING CLAY

What would a list of modeling activities be without mentioning modeling clay? When children play with clay or play-dough they can show each other how to roll, pull, cut, pinch, stretch and mold the dough into an infinite variety of shapes and scenes.

There are many types of modeling clay: You may be able to dig clay right out of the ground and you can purchase inexpensive clay from a potter or from an art shop. Play-dough is easy to make at home.

Play-dough is easy to make at home.

Homemade Modeling Clay

Here is a recipe that does not require any cooking.

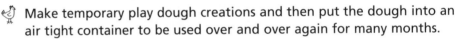

Mix together:

    2 cups of flour

    1 cup of salt

    a couple of spoonfuls of cooking oil

    3/4 cup of water

Divide the dough into several lumps and add food coloring, different flavors of koolaid or melted crayons to make beautiful colors.

- Make temporary play dough creations and then put the dough into an air tight container to be used over and over again for many months.

- Make permanent play-dough figures by baking play-dough in a low oven for about an hour. Then, the next time you get together, everyone can paint their creations.

Edible Modeling Clay

Cookie dough makes great edible modeling clay. One good tasting recipe is:

    1 cup of a mixture of brown sugar, white sugar and honey (1/3 cup of each)

    1/3 cup of butter

    1 egg

    1 teaspoon of vanilla

Mix all this together with:

    2-3 cups of flour

    1 teaspoon of baking soda

    1 teaspoon of salt

Mix well and chill in the refrigerator for at least an hour (it will keep fresh for up to a week). To make sure the cookies are safe to eat, children need to remember to wash and dry their hands carefully. Sprinkling hands with flour keeps the dough from getting sticky. Place creations on a baking sheet and paint them with **Egg Yolk Paint** before baking them for 8-10 minutes at 375 degrees.

Egg Yolk Paint

is made by mixing up an egg yolk, and dividing it into several small containers (an egg carton works very well). Add a different drop of food coloring to each container to make bright colors. If the paint thickens, add a few drops of water. Apply the paint with thin paint brushes. Encourage children to copy each other's designs.

ORIGAMI

MODELING

Origami is the Japanese art of paper folding. In Japan children learn origami at their mothers' knees by watching closely, listening carefully and then carrying out the instructions with neatness and accuracy. Re-creating origami patterns is like singing and dancing because the pleasure comes in sharing the same beautiful work of art again and again. Origami gives children a cross-cultural opportunity to practice patience, focus energy and produce results they are proud of. Rooted in Asia, origami reflects the ingenuity and aesthetics of Japanese culture. Working together to fold a thousand cranes helps end war and build world peace. You can learn origami from a book, but it is much more satisfying and fun to learn from others who know one or more of the thousands of figures that can be created by carefully folding paper.

MIRROR, MIRROR

Mirror games are one of the foundation games of improvisational drama. In the basic game, two people face each other and one person becomes the mirror, trying to exactly copy the facial expressions, movements, postures and mimed actions of the other person.

See if your community center will let you take the children into the dance studio for an hour!

- Children can play this game in a large group with everyone mirroring one person.
- Play in pairs or in two lines facing each other.
- Play this game while standing in front of a real mirror. See if your community center will let you take the children into the dance studio for an hour!

Some children are very comfortable and skilled at mirroring, other children are much more comfortable being the one looking into the mirror. Switch back and forth and change partners often.

IMITATING NATURE

This is a quiet, reflective activity in which each child finds a place outside to sit quietly for about five minutes.

PSST! I THINK WE ARE BEING COPIED.

- The first step is to relax.
- The second step is to observe the surrounding sensations: sights, sounds, movements, smells, touches.
- The third step is to imitate one or more of these sights, sounds, movements or physical sensations.
- The fourth step is to gather together and show what you each learned from your natural teachers.

The result should be a greater awareness of how much there is to learn by carefully observing the natural world of which we are an integral part.

BREAKING THE ICE

A group of us were exploring disability differences. Alicia broke the ice by showing us the ways she could use her elbows to do things that most people do with their hands. The more we put our elbows together, the more easily we laughed together. Sandra discovered that she could draw bouquets of flowers on the blackboard. Mary was able to eat an entire slice of pie with her fork clasped firmly between her elbows. Toby managed to turn the door handle so that we could all go out to play a game of elbow-ball. As we opened up to exploring the abilities Alicia had developed through her life of living with arms that ended at the elbows, we opened up to celebrating all of our talents. The tensions and uncertainties about our differences shattered into thousands of beautiful gems.

by Sheena Nichols, age 10

The Mitten

One freezing wintry day, a little mouse found a mitten lying on the ground and crept inside for shelter.

Soon a cold frog came upon the mitten too. *"Can I come in and get warm?"*
"Yes, you may," said the mouse. And so the frog hopped in.

After a while a rabbit came shivering down the path. *"May I share your cozy house?"*
"You are welcome to come on in," said the mouse and the frog. And so the rabbit dug his way in.

A little later, a frigid fox noticed the mitten as he was trotting down the path. *"Please let me in."*
"Oh, I think we can make room," said the mouse, frog and rabbit. The fox burrowed right into the middle.

Suddenly, a wild boar with icicles hanging from his tusks almost ran over the mitten. *"Oh, may I take shelter in your cozy home?"* *"Certainly you may,"* said the mouse, frog, rabbit and fox. The boar pawed his way in.

Before they had any time to settle down again, a bear almost stepped on the mitten. *"I am so cold, I can't sleep. Oh if only I could cuddle up in your cave!"*

"Well, why not?" said the mouse, frog, rabbit, fox and wild boar. And the bear squirmed his way in.

By now there were six animals in the mitten. They were very, very warm, but they were so tightly packed that no one could move and they could hardly breathe. Later that day, as Farmer Dido was returning from the barn, he discovered his lost mitten lying on the forest path.

"Oh my, I am a lucky man!" he cried as he picked up his mitten and shook it out vigorously. Out tumbled the mouse, frog, rabbit, fox, wild boar and the bear.

"Oh it feels good to be free!" they cried as they danced off into the forest together. With both hands toasty warm again, Farmer Dido whistled merrily all the way home.

(A UKRAINIAN FOLK TALE)

SKILL 3: BREAKING THE ICE

BREAKING THE ICE

Have you ever gone on a walk down a country road after a frost? Kids of all ages love breaking the ice that forms inside the puddles and seeing the beautiful patterns that emerge. Beautiful patterns also emerge during activities that break up the ice in a frozen group of children. There are many ways of warming the atmosphere, building interest and energizing a group so that children can release tension and melt away nervousness. As children relax, they open up their hearts and minds to each other. Breaking the ice is a juggling act because you are simultaneously building trust, engaging everyone's interest and helping everyone to connect.

- 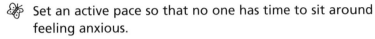 Set an active pace so that no one has time to sit around feeling anxious.
- Get everyone involved in activities that are interesting and fun.
- Learn and remember everyone's names.
- Get everyone laughing together.
- Show that this is a safe and welcoming group.
- Mix and match people.

there are many ways of warming the atmosphere, building interest and energizing a group.

You have a responsibility to return the trust children are placing in you by interacting in ways that are safe without being boring, challenging without being threatening, interesting without being scary and bonding without pushing everyone too close for comfort. After children get to know each other they enjoy playing ice breaker games again and again to release tension or re-energize the group.

 A strong word of caution: *Some children and adults have had bad experiences with so-called "ice breaker" activities that were so "touchy-feely" that they felt physically or emotionally uncomfortable, so confrontive that they felt invaded, or so competitive that they felt like failures. Games and learning activities that cross social boundaries, invade privacy, confront weak spots, or set children up to fail may (or may not) have their time and place in counseling or life skills training programs, but they are **not** ice breakers.*

Many of the games and activities that go with Skills 1 and 2 are great ice breakers. Here are some more cooperative games, creative activities and nature adventures that quickly get kids relaxed and happy to be getting to know each other.

SWITCH CHAIRS

This is my favorite name game. Remove your chair so that there is one less chair than the number of people in the room. Stand in the middle of the room and say "When I call out your name, stand up." (For example, "Carrie, Ken, Beau, Singaru, Eva"). Once a few people are standing, say "switch chairs." As they are switching you sit down in an empty chair. One person will be left standing. It is now that person's turn to call out a few names and then sit down in an empty chair. It is just fine to point to someone and ask, "What is your name?" if you don't remember. Play until everyone's name gets called out at least once. Here are a couple of variations.

Play until everyone's name gets called out at least once.

- Remove two chairs so that a pair of people call out names.

- Ask people to stand up and switch chairs based on what they have in common: Everyone who likes hip hop music, everyone with white on their shoes, everyone with freckles, everyone who was born here, everyone who likes ice cream, everyone who takes a bus to school, etc.

TOSSED SALAD NAME GAME

This is an old classic that children of all ages seem to love so long as it doesn't feel like a memory test and so long as there is not too much sitting around waiting. Each person gives their name and the name of a fruit or vegetable. If you want, the fruit or vegetable could start with the same letter as the person's name. After everyone gives their name and food association, participants take turns helping each other to remember everyone's name and associated fruit or vegetable.

- Instead of making a salad, your group can think of associations for going on a picnic, packing a suitcase, travelling to outer space, living in the forest or any other category you want.

- Once you have finished learning names through association, you can combine this game with the **Switch Chairs** game above and really get blended.

NAME JAM

Go around the circle and help each other clap, tap and/or march out a distinctive rhythm or action for the syllables in each persons first, middle and last name. Now, have a "name jam" where you call out a first name and then everyone claps out the rhythm, call out another name and everyone claps out the rhythm and so on. It is amazing how relaxed everyone gets as they clap and how well they all remember each other's names from then on. Also see **Rhythm And Movement Jam Sessions** (page 87).

DO YOU KNOW YOUR NEIGHBORS?

This is a name exchange variation on the traditional game called **Do You Love Your Neighbor?** Everyone sits in a circle. One person goes in the middle, spins around, points to someone and asks "Do you know your neighbors?" That person makes one of three choices.

BREAKING THE ICE

🦋 CHOICE 1: They could say "No, but I would like to meet them." The two people on either side stand up and introduce themselves. They stay standing after they get introduced. The person in the middle points to someone else and asks, "Do you know your neighbors?"   OR,

MY NEIGHBORS ARE OUT VISITING RIGHT NOW

🦋 CHOICE 2: They could say "Yes" and introduce the two people on either side to the group. "This is _____ and this is _____." They stay standing after they get introduced. The person in the middle points to someone else and asks, "Do you know your neighbors?"   OR,

🦋 CHOICE 3: They could say "My neighbors are out visiting right now, could you come back later?" This is a signal for EVERYONE who has been introduced so far (everyone standing) to change places. The last person to get to a new place goes in the middle, points to someone else and asks, "Do you know your neighbors?"

SHAKE HANDS!

This is a good ice-breaker when there are people in the group who communicate in different ways. In the simplest form of this game, each child goes around the room and shakes hands with every person in the group. There are many rules that can be added.

🦋 Shake hands, smile and make eye contact with each person for at least five seconds.

🦋 Shake hands with one person and then keep shaking hands until you connect with another person with your other hand.

🦋 Shake hands then introduce yourselves through mime and gesture.

🦋 Find a partner and together shake hands with all the other pairs; while trying to learn the names of every other pair in the room.

🦋 Shake hands one way with the first person, two different ways with the second person, three different ways with the third person and so on.

ROLL CALL

Everyone stands in a circle. The goal is for each person to call out their name, one at a time, in random order without interrupting. The challenge is that you start off by turning around and facing away from each other. Once you call out your name, you turn back to face the circle. When everyone has called out their name and you are all turned around, you are done. If two people call out their name at the same time, everyone turns back around and tries again. This game is extremely funny in a frustrating sort of way and is best played as an ice breaker with children who already know each other's names.

Roll Call is extremely funny in a frustrating sort of way.

BREAKING
THE ICE

Children who
can wink,
cross their eyes,
wiggle their ears
or roll their
tongues add a new
dimension to
ice breaker
activities.

SCREAM

Everyone stands in a circle looking down at their toes. The leader calls (in a voice of terror and pending doom) "Look out!!!!!" Everyone looks up at someone. If no one is looking back, that person puts their head back down and covers their ears. If two people are looking at each other, they both let out a blood curdling scream and then quickly put their heads down until the leader calls out "Look out" again. If you don't want to disturb everyone, you can play these quieter variations.

- **Teeter-totter:** When two people are looking at each other one sits down and the other stands up. (This is easier said than done.)
- **Faces:** When two people are looking at each other they make funny faces and try to look down again before laughing.
- **Stare Down:** Stare at each other until one person looks away or laughs. (Children who can wink, cross their eyes, wiggle their ears or roll their tongues add a new dimension to ice breaker activities such as this game.)

WEB OF LIKES

This is an easy variation on **Web of Life** activities. Sit or stand in a circle and build a web of interconnections. Hold a ball of wool in your hand and say "My name is _____ and I like _____ (an activity). Who else likes _____?" For example, I might say, "My name is Linda and I like bicycling. Who else likes bicycling?" I hold on to the yarn and throw the ball of wool to someone who likes that activity and that person says, "My name is _____ and I like _____ (another activity). Who else likes _____?" As the game goes on the children will become connected by a web of yarn. As the web is being built people often see connections with a spider web, stars or other natural patterns. When someone tugs on one part of the web, other people are affected. Building a web has infinite possibilities for learning about our connections to each other and to the earth. Michael Cohen (page 157) and Joseph Cornell (page 158) both teach many variations on **Web of Life** activities.

*Cowichan Valley Naturalist Society playing a **Web of Life** game.*

GLOBAL VILLAGE GAME

Sit around a map of the world on the table or on the floor. Make play dough models of places you have lived and travelled, places your relatives live and places your parents, grandparents and ancestors came from. Take turns exchanging stories about your connections around the world.

FAMILY TREE

This game, that is best played under a real tree, helps children quickly learn about each other's family backgrounds. Children get into partners or small groups. Each pair receives a large sheet of paper, a felt marker and a different "Family Tree" question. Here are some sample questions.

- What countries do you and your parents come from?
- What languages are spoken in your home?
- What places have you lived?
- What is your favorite holiday or celebration?
- What is a favorite meal in your family?
- What is your favorite song?
- What is the most watched movie or television program in your family?
- What is something different about your family?
- What pets do you have in your family?
- How many people live in your home?
- What is a favorite saying in your family?

Each pair finds another pair, interviews them and writes down the answers without writing down names of who gave the answer. Then they interview another pair and another until everyone has been interviewed or until the time is up. If two people give the same answer, just write it down once. When the interviewing is finished, the answers are hung from the branches of the tree with tape and string. Now the pairs explore the "Family Tree," reading the answers and guessing who said what. Finally, everyone gets back in a large circle and finds out who goes with what answer. There is always a lot of good-natured laughter and expressions of surprise as the children get to know each other's backgrounds.

there is always a lot of good-natured laughter and expressions of surprise as the children get to know each other's backgrounds.

SNOW BALL FIGHT

Hand out paper and pencils and ask each person to answer several simple introductory questions such as these examples.

- What is your favorite color?
- What season were you born in?
- What sport do you enjoy the most?
- If you were a famous person who would you be?

Now, everyone crumples their paper up into a ball. When everyone is ready, someone calls out "Snow Ball Fight" and everyone throws paper balls at each other until everyone is laughing helplessly. Now each person takes turns opening a snow ball, reading the answers out loud and trying to guess who wrote those answers.

My partner renamed the Snowball Fight game "Smorgasbord" and had a crumpled paper "food fight" that was a lot of fun!

BREAKING THE ICE

the ice will quickly melt as you eat together.

ASK EACH OTHER QUESTIONS

This is an ice breaker that works well for small groups. Children write down interview questions that will give other children a chance to talk about their background and experience. Put the cards in a pile. Spin a bottle to select someone to ask the question. Spin the bottle again to select who will answer the question.

NACHOS

Make a group snack that all goes on one large plate and has to be dipped such as nachos, vegetables and dip, or fruit fondue. The ice will quickly melt as you eat together.

THREE WAY SCULPTURES

Select several three-way sculptures to make. Here are some popular formations.

- **Monkey:** The person in the middle makes a monkey face. The two on either side make monkey gestures with their outside arms.
- **Giraffe:** The person in the middle stretches his arms up to show a long neck. The two on either side stand on one foot and lean inwards to each become one of the giraffe's long legs.
- **Elephant:** The person in the middle uses his arms to make an elephant's trunk. The two on either side put their outside arms on their hips to make elephant ears.
- **Bicycle:** The person in the middle steers, the two on either side pedal the air with their outside leg.
- **Train:** The person in the middle pulls the train horn. The two on either side show the wheels going around with their outer arm. Everyone says "Choo Choo."
- **Boat:** The person in the middle raises the sail. The two on either side paddle.
- **Airplane:** The person in the middle makes a propeller go around. The two on either side make wings with their outside arms.
- **Your Invention:** Create your own 3-way sculptures.

Now one child goes in the middle, spins around, points to someone and says one of the statue names (such as **Giraffe!**). That person and the people on either side quickly form the statue together. Once they have accomplished this feat, one of them volunteers to exchange places, go in the middle to spin around, point and say another statue name.

GUIDED TOUR

Divide into small groups and select tour guides to give guided tours of the area you are in. This is a great way to break the ice when welcoming new children into any group, visitors to an exchange program, new campers, new students or new neighbors.

WELCOME MAT

Making a welcome mat shows the diversity of a group. Place pie plates of paint, paint brushes and other art supplies around the edge of a big strip of mural paper or an old sheet. (Put another old sheet, a tarp or newspaper underneath to prevent spills on to the floor or carpet.) Make a welcoming mural of thumbprints, handprints, signatures, pictures, favorite sayings and greetings in many languages and styles.

BREAKING THE ICE

Make a welcoming mural of thumbprints, handprints, signatures, pictures, favorite sayings and greetings in many languages and styles.

NATURE SHOUT

Sit outside in a circle and look all around. As soon as someone notices something interesting, they go into the middle of the circle, call out what they noticed and sit back down as quickly as possible. For example, someone notices a falling leaf. They go in the middle, call out "falling leaf!" run back and sit down. If two or more people arrive in the middle of the circle at the same time, they call out what they noticed at the same time and then switch places.

PARTICIPATORY PACING

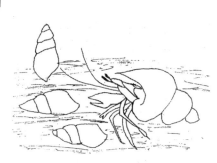

Hermit Crab sat in the shade of a breadfruit tree, singing out his song of happiness while Sea Eagle jeered from the branches above. *"What could you possibly have to sing about from such a low place way down there on the same level with the ground?"*

"You can look down on me all you want, but you can't make me ashamed of my beautiful voice," Hermit Crab replied.

Sea Eagle scoffed at that. *"You might be a great singer, but you are so small and the house on your back is so heavy, you aren't much good for anything else. If I challenge you to a race from this tree to the end of the beach and back again, I will get back before you have a chance to move more than a few inches."*

"You're on!" sang out Hermit Crab. *"The race starts at sunrise tomorrow morning."* Sea Eagle screeched with laughter so loudly that he didn't notice Hermit Crab sing out a message that was relayed from crab to crab to crab all along the beach. *"Tomorrow, when you look up and see Eagle flying over, be sure to sing out, 'Here I am, in your shadow.'"*

The next day, just as the sun rose above the horizon, Hermit Crab crawled out of his house at the bottom of the tree and sang out, *"Here I am, in your shadow."*

"Not for long you aren't," squawked Sea Eagle and he took off like a shot. But no matter how hard and fast he flew he couldn't get ahead of Hermit Crab's song. All the way along the beach and all the way back he heard, *"Here I am, in your shadow,"* down below him. And when he landed once again in the branches of the breadfruit tree, Hermit Crab was already there singing his song of happiness in the cool shade below.

"I guess I've got a few things to learn from you," admitted Sea Eagle. And so Hermit Crab began giving Sea Eagle singing lessons.

(A SOLOMON ISLANDS FOLK TALE)

What's your favorite kind of breakfast shake? How about a banana, strawberry and yogurt combo? That's the mixture the students who have home-room in the cooking room choose most mornings at their school. It only takes a couple of minutes to chop up all the ingredients and throw them into the blender. Everyone waits in great anticipation as Randy gets ready to hit his head-switch and turn the blender on. Sometimes he takes his time to turn the switch off again and sometimes he is as fast as lightning. He uses his eyes to select a helper to fill the glasses and the kids who were on time are the first in line to get their breakfast. Whether it pours out smooth or lumpy it always tastes good. Everyone toasts another day of knowing each other and someone always volunteers to fill the dishwasher.

by Wong Wei, age 13

Participatory hikes are as much fun for the children who mosey along with the caterpillars as for children who fly ahead with the butterflies!

SKILL 4: PARTICIPATORY PACING

Participatory pacing is a key skill for getting kids actively involved. Pacing helps children make smooth transitions through the stages of every game and activity. Pace yourself as you count to ten.

1. Gather together.

2. Get oriented.

3. Participate actively.

4. Share the leadership.

5. Do a midway assessment of how it's going.

6. Finish up.

7. Debrief.

8. Clean up.

9. Take a deep breath.

10. Shift to the next activity.

Participatory pacing is comfortably challenging. Children have enough time to get involved and take turns. They have adequate time to make the transition from one phase of the activity to the next, but no one is left sitting around waiting with nothing to do.

Inclusive leaders adjust the pace by paying close attention to feedback from the group and from individuals within the group. Activities are extended if everyone is very involved and they are shortened or changed if most of the participants in the group seem to need a break.

PARTICIPATORY PACING

Adjust the pace by paying close attention to feedback from the group and from individuals within the group.

Tip: Inclusive leaders are flexible enough to individualize the pacing according to different children's needs. A child with a shorter attention span is allowed to move onto the next phase of an activity early if needed, or to do another aspect of the activity. A child who needs a longer period of time is allowed to start an activity early, continue longer, or is given help to keep up.

PARTICIPATORY PACING

Children can take turns leading these games.

Here are several cooperative games and creative activities that give children enjoyable opportunities to practice participatory pacing indoors and out. Children can take turns leading these games and supporting individual children to get more actively involved.

Hide And Seek Games

The many variations of hide and seek games are excellent ways for group leaders to practice participatory pacing while the kids have a great time. Start your stop watch and go!

1. *Gathering Together:* Before the first minute is up you have gathered everyone together.

2. *Get Oriented:* Before the second minute ends you have reviewed the hide and seek rules and agreed on the boundaries.

3. & 4. *Active Participation and Shared Leadership:* Before the third minute is up seekers have closed their eyes, hiders have hidden and the start of the search has been signalled.

5. *Midway Assessment:* Before five minutes have gone by you have assessed how the game is going and taken any action needed to help the pace along. Sometimes it's going perfectly, but sometimes the seekers need a little extra help.

6. *Finish up:* Everyone is found while everyone is still intently involved! No one has even thought of wandering off or suggested playing another game.

7. *Debrief:* It takes less than a minute to listen to any comments and find out if the kids want to play again. If they do, great — start another game! If not, shift to another activity quickly and smoothly.

8. *Clean up:* Put away the tin can or any other equipment and you are done!

9. & 10. *Take a Deep Breath and Shift* …to the next adventure!

Here are several well-loved hide and seek games.

Sardines: In this game everyone counts (to about thirty) while one or two people hide (the first of what will soon be many sardines). After everyone else finishes counting, players wander around looking for the sardines. When players find the hiding spot, they quietly climb in and hide there too. When everyone is jammed in like sardines in a tin, it's time to select another couple of hiders and start the counting again.

Kick the Can: One person kicks a can as far away as they can. Everyone runs and hides while "It" gets the can and sets it up on the home base. Now "It" tries to find the hiders. They must come out when their name and hiding place is called and sit in the home base. In the meantime, other children try to free them by sneaking home and kicking the can. In this cooperative version, the successful kicker stays behind to help the person who is "It".

Camouflage: Camouflage (or **Thicket**) is one of the finest hide and seek games around, especially when it is played at dusk or in a forest. A couple of owls hide their eyes and count to twenty while the mice and rabbits scatter to their holes and thickets. They must still be able to see the owls, even when they are hiding. When they have finished counting, the owls call out "LOOKING!" The owls can't move their feet but they can move their heads all around, looking for the mice. The owls call out the names and hiding places of anyone they can see and those mice and rabbits come in and sit down in the owl's den.

When the owls can't see anymore mice, they call out "NUMBER!" and hold up one hand each, signalling a number between two and ten. The mice and rabbits must be able to see the number (they may need to peek out from behind a tree or even creep in to a better spot). The owls call out the names and hiding places of any mice or rabbits they can see and those animals come in to sit down in the owl's den.

Now the mice and rabbits who have been found, call out the hiding places of any mice or rabbits still camouflaged. The owls identify those animals and call them into to their nest. The last mice or rabbits come in and tell the secret number. If they are right, they get to be the next owls.

Follow That Cab!

Everyone helps keep up the pace in this tag game for a large group (also called **Streets and Roads**). Two children take on the role of cars in a car chase. One more person takes on the role of the traffic director. The rest of the children make a "city" by facing forward and lining up in several rows. In each row, children stand side by side with their arms stretched out and finger tips touching. The game works well if there are about the same number of lines as there are rows of children (for example: 25 children would be 5 children in 5 rows. 35 children would be about 6 children in 6 rows).

One car starts chasing the other car, back and forth along the rows of children (the streets). Going through arms is not allowed. Suddenly, the traffic director calls out "Roads!" and all the children turn a quarter turn to their right side. The cars continue to chase each other on these roads that are now all going side-ways. Just as suddenly the traffic director calls out "Streets!" and all the children turn a quarter left turn back to the front.

The result is a wild and whacky, fast-paced chase through the streets with lots of opportunities for children to take turns being cars, traffic director or the streets and roads of fast-paced city life.

Everyone helps keep up the pace in this fast-moving tag game for a large group.

If the car being chased is extremely speedy, then add a couple more cars into the chase so that children get turns quickly.

If the car being chased moves slowly, then the traffic director can help out by calling out "Streets!" or "Roads!" at strategic moments that block the chase car.

PARTICIPATORY PACING

Go Go Go STOP

Pacing is the essence of this game that my grandmother liked to play over and over when she was a little girl in Northern England. (City children call it **Green Light, Red Light** but it is the same game). Everyone lines up on one side of an open area. One person (the traffic director) goes to the other side of the area, closes their eyes and starts saying, "Go, go, go... stop." As soon as saying "Stop" (but not before) the traffic director quickly looks up. In the meantime, everyone has tried to move up a few steps but be as frozen as ice before the traffic director looks up. The traffic director calls to anyone who is still moving, "_____ (say the name or ask the name to learn it) "Go, go, go BACK." That child moves back, a few steps or all the way back depending on what the group has decided the rule will be. The traffic director continues until someone makes it right across to the other side, then that person becomes the new traffic director. Now everyone runs back to the beginning and starts all over again.

 Instead of changing places, the new traffic directors join the traffic director and they jointly set the "Go, Go, Go Stop" pace and help each other detect moving vehicles.

 Play in pairs or small groups to even the odds so that everyone will have a chance to be a traffic director.

Whoever–Whatever!

This fast moving after-lunch wake up game gets people moving and laughing as they explore the different gifts they each contribute to the group. Prepare a list of characteristics that will connect various members of the group, and acknowledge some individual gifts. Add in an easy, fun and non-threatening action to go with each characteristic. Call the instructions out, keeping a fast pace and ending with an instruction that includes everyone in the group. This activity works best if you design it to match the characteristics of the children in your group. These instructions are only examples.

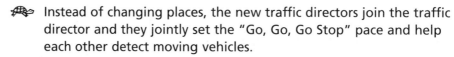 Whoever has lived here all their lives come into the center and join hands.

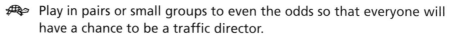 Whoever plays football do a push up.

Whoever likes music come in the middle and sing a song together.

Whoever speaks Punjabi, come in the middle and count to 10 in that language.

Whoever has a pet make the sound that your pet makes.

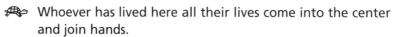 Whoever likes pizza show how you spin one over your head.

End with an instruction that everyone has in common such as:

Whoever is in this group come in the circle, raise your hands and shout "Hooray!"

this after-lunch wake up game gets people moving and laughing as they explore the different gifts they each contribute to the group.

Going On A Lion Safari

Get everyone involved in action stories that start at a steady pace, build suspense and end up by running all the way back to the beginning as quickly as you can go. Going on a lion safari is a popular favorite, but you can follow this format to make up any story. The lion safari story goes like this:

PARTICIPATORY PACING

Hey everyone, let's go see if we can find us a LION today!

Let's get ready. Pack your lunch (*slap hands together*).

Grab your camera (*click tongue while miming taking a picture*).

Go out the door (*open and shut hands*).

Walk down the path (*tap hands left-right on your knees*).

Oh, oh, here's a field of tall grass. We can't jump over it, can't go around it, can't get under it, guess we will just go through it (*rub hands back and forth to make a swishing sound*).

Here's the trail. Let's keep walking (*stomp feet or tap hands left-right on your knees*).

Oh, oh, here's a river. We can't go around it, can't get under it, it's rushing too fast to go through it. We'll have to jump over it. Ready, set… (*one big clap or jump, then pause and make a second big clap or jump*).

You can follow this format to make up any story.

Did everyone make it? I didn't even get my shoes wet. Here's the trail. Let's keep walking (*stomp feet or tap hands left-right on your knees*).

Oh, oh, here's a swamp filled with quicksand. Can't jump over it, can't get under it, can't go through it, guess we'll have to pick our way around the edges of it (*point your fingers down or stand on your tiptoes as you demonstrate stepping carefully around the swamp. Making squishing noises with your mouth enhances the effect*).

Here's the trail. Let's keep walking (*stomp feet or tap hands left-right on your knees*).

Oh, no, here's a big gigantic cliff. Can't jump over it, can't get under it, can't go through it. Guess we'll have to climb it (*mime climbing a cliff and make huffing, puffing sounds to show how challenging it is*).

Don't look down or your knees will start shaking. Is everyone up and over the edge? Whew, we didn't lose anyone! Here's the trail. Let's keep walking (*tap hands left-right on your knees*).

Oh, wow, we are almost at the top of this gigantic mountain. I think we are as high as Mt. Everest. If we just go around that rock there we'll get a good view of the valley on the other side (*tap hands left-right on your knees, slow down and hesitate*).

(*In a startled voice*) There's more than a view on the other side of that rock… there's a **LION!**

Now go through the trip backwards as fast as you and the children can do it:

Take a quick picture (*click tongue while miming taking a picture*).

Go back round the rock (*tap hands left-right on your knees*).

Down the mountain (*mime climbing a cliff and make huffing, puffing sounds*).

Run along the trail (*tap hands left-right on your knees*).

Around the swamp (*step carefully with pointed fingers while making squishing sounds*).

Jump over the river (*one big clap, then pause and make a second big clap*).

Through the grass (*rub hands back and forth to make a swishing sound*).

Along the path, don't look back. I think we are being followed (*tap hands left-right on your knees*)!

In the door, shut it and lock it (*open and shut hands*)!

Home sweet home, Let's eat (*slap hands together, clap for the ending and take a bow*).

PARTICIPATORY PACING

Inclusive Assembly Line

This challenging variation on **Cooperative Drawing** (page 23) emphasizes pacing and rhythm. Unlike factory assembly lines that turn out identical products, the goal of an inclusive assembly line is to produce a set of cooperatively produced, individually unique creations. Everyone sits around the edges of a long table; banquet style. Each person except one has some art supplies that can all be mixed and matched together.

- For a simple assembly line, each person could have a lump of play dough of different colors.

- For a more complicated assembly line, a couple of people could have play dough and others might have decorations such as feathers, drinking straws, beads, construction paper and pipe-cleaners. Use your imagination.

- One of the silliest times I played this game, each person was given a piece of bubble gum to chew, a plate to put it on and a toothpick to sculpt with.

The person who begins without any art supplies is the first timekeeper. He or she calls out "Start assembling!" and everyone begins to create an art project. As soon as the timekeeper calls out "Move down the assembly line!" each person passes their work of art to the left and people add their creativity to the emerging art object. The person without any art is the new timekeeper and decides when to call out "Move down the assembly line!"

- To make things even more challenging, the timekeeper can vary the direction of the assembly line by calling out "Pass across the assembly line" or "Workers, switch places." (Everyone leaves the art where it is and moves to a different seat.)

- When one of the timekeepers calls out "Coffee Break", everyone can walk around and admire their individually produced products, and decide whether it is time to continue or time to end the shift!

Participatory Hikes

Setting an inclusive pace on a hike or outing is an enjoyable and creative adventure for a connected group of children. Getting over barriers to even go on the hike or outing is the first challenge. Look for creative alternatives to the more usual strategies of leaving some children behind. Setting a pace is the second challenge. How can all the children have fun without setting a pace that is too fast for some or too slow for others? Figuring out how everyone can have an enjoyable outing is all part of the fun when you are exploring diversity. Different groups of people will come up with different answers.

- One group I was part of decided to go on a **Piggy-Back Hike** with the bigger kids carrying some of the smaller children.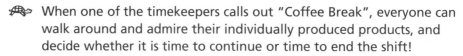

- Another group went on a **Dare To Be Different Walk**. Each person adjusted their pace by taking the walk in a different way. Stilts, hula hoops, skipping ropes, juggling balls and walking backwards were especially popular on this short outing.

Figuring out how everyone can have an enjoyable outing is all part of the fun when you are exploring diversity.

Another group took a **Tote-And-Carry Walk**. They got into groups of four. Two linked arms in a rescuer's carry that they had been wanting to use ever since they had learned it in their Scout group, one sat on their arms and got to go for the ride. One walked along carrying a backpack with water, snacks and first aid supplies.

Groups often decide to go on a hike or outing with several **Different Destinations**. Some people might go up a mountain, others to the park, others to the store, others to the beach and a few might want to go on an armchair journey in the living room. They meet back at a designated time and all share their experiences.

One group I was with decided to go on an **Access Walk** around town. They marked down all the access barriers they could find and brainstormed ways of solving them. Several of the group members had disabilities and so they were experts in opening people's eyes to the inaccessible places. Also see **Access Check** (page 142).

One group went on a hike in their neighborhood, from **Home To Home**, visiting each of their families.

Sam Sullivan in Vancouver, BC invented **Cross-Country Wheelchairs** so that people with mobility disabilities and people interested in disability issues could hike together along the many mountain trails that surround this corner of Canada. They learned that solving one problem can lead to others — no matter how maneuverable the chair is, the person being pushed through the rain, snow and sleet common in this part of the world, runs a much higher risk of catching hypothermia than the people doing the pushing!

Another group made the hike into a **Ribbon Chase**. This took a whole day to organize. Several kids went ahead to lay out a mile-long route and mark each choice point with a ribbon tied to a tree or under a rock. Then, in the afternoon, everyone set out. The kids who liked to run were able to go two or three times as far as everyone else because their role was to scout ahead to search out the ribbon and then run back to guide everyone to the goal. Once everyone arrived at a choice point, the ribbon was collected and the scouts ran on to find the next ribbon. (Ribbon chases originated in England. They are also known as **Paper Chases**, **Flour Chases** and the **Hash**).

the kids who liked to run were able to go two or three times as far as everyone else.

Several groups I have been involved in have gone on **Camping Trips**. Sometimes we camp close enough that children who prefer their own bed can go home at night and come back in the morning.

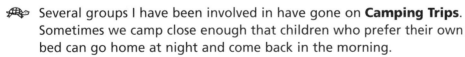

I'LL BE YOUR PARTNER

In the process of figuring out his own learning disability that made writing and spelling difficult, ten-year-old Tony developed a keen interest in (and compassion toward) other children's differences. He was able to put his academic frustrations in the background, and practice his gifts for getting along with everyone in his class. His enthusiasm for others was like a spark that made every game and activity into an especially fun time. Everyone always wanted to sit by Tony, work with Tony and play with Tony. At the same time, Tony was always willing to sit, work and play with everyone who asked him. When I asked for his secret formula, he said, *"To me it's all about learning to be respectful; just being respectful to each other."*

Children in the Dell (FOLLOW THE SAME TUNE AND RULES AS "FARMER IN THE DELL")

Children in the dell, Children in the dell
Big, small, short, tall, children in the dell

Bravest goes first, bravest goes first
Big, small, short, tall, bravest goes first.

First finds one older, first finds one older
Big, small, short, tall, first finds one older

Old picks young, old picks young
Big, small, short, tall, old picks young.

Young gets help from strong, young gets help from strong
Big, small, short, tall, young gets help from strong.

Strong goes with brave, strong goes with brave
Big, small, short, tall, strong goes with brave.

(Go back to the beginning of the song and start the game over)

by 吴佳辰, age 9

"I Danced with the Kids"
by Danika Carlson, age 4

SKILL 5: I'LL BE YOUR PARTNER!

I'LL BE YOUR PARTNER

Think of all the times children are asked to find a partner or divide into small groups. Instead of just sticking to one or two best friends, children who are exploring diversity together take turns being everyone's partner. There are actually two connecting skills involved in being a partner.

- The first is learning to say "Will you be my partner?" to other people.

- The second is learning to assess the invitation and say, "Yes, I'll be your partner" so long as it feels safe.

the skill of being a welcoming partner is a very powerful force in any group.

The skill of being a welcoming partner is a very powerful force in any group because children are no longer forming exclusive cliques or attempting to gain popularity by rejecting children who are different. All games and activities can be adapted so that children are supporting each other in partners or small groups instead of participating as individuals.

- Inclusive leaders think up creative ways of matching children into partners by chance or on the basis of differences rather than their similarities.

- Inclusive leaders also support children in the background and on the sidelines to more easily find partners.

- Leaders often ask children to find a buddy when they go out in the community, out in nature or swimming. Each partner in a buddy relationship needs to have the ability to meet their partner's basic social needs for safety, equality, choice and fun.

Tip: Three-way partnerships work well to support children who are not yet able to take on full responsibility for meeting another person's basic social needs. In a three-way partnership, a person with inclusive leadership skills partners with a child who needs extra support and they find a third partner together. Forming three-way partnerships is an excellent way for one-on-one support workers to support the child they are with to find a buddy instead of just partnering with the child and inadvertently isolating him or her from the other children.

I'LL BE YOUR PARTNER

Here are several cooperative games, creative activities and experiences in nature that give children enjoyable opportunities to practice the skill of "I'll be your partner!"

Find A Partner

Explore different ways of finding partners.

Explore different ways of finding partners.

- **Touch Search:** Everybody closes their eyes and finds a partner by touch.

- **Whose Is This?:** Everybody puts something of theirs in a pile in the middle of the room. With eyes closed, find an object. With eyes open, match the object to its owner and you have found your new partner.

- **Hat Trick:** Children pick numbers out of a hat. Each child finds the person who has a number on either side of their number. For example a child who selects number 8 could partner with number 7, number 9 or both.

- **Opposites Attract** (also see page 122): Find a partner with a difference such as different colored eyes, different height, different shoe size, different hair or skin color, different age, different birth month or different gender.

- **Flip A Coin:** Each person has a coin. Move around the room flipping coins with people. If they match you have found your partner. If they are different, you move on to flip coins with another person.

- **Scissors, Paper, Rock:** Everybody moves around the room playing Scissors, Paper, Rock with each other. If they match, the children have found their partner. If they don't match, both children move on to play Scissors, Paper, Rock with another person.

> **Scissors, Paper, Rock** is a game in which two children face each other and shake one fist up and down in time to the chant, "Scissors, Paper, Rock… Scissors, Paper, Rock… Scissors, Paper, Rock." After the third chant, they simultaneously make their hand into one of three shapes:
>
> Scissors – pointer finger and middle finger make scissors
>
> Paper – flat hand
>
> Rock – hand stays in a fist
>
> Scissors cut paper. Paper covers rocks. Rocks crush scissors.

All Aboard

Here is game that I learned when I was about six years old. There was a teacher who didn't yell at the bad kids during recess and lunch. Instead, she always turned herself into a train and said, "Come on aboard" to any of us who wanted to play. When she had enough kids, she would get a game of tag, hide-and-seek or dodge ball going. Pretty soon, we learned to make our own trains that welcomed everyone on board even when she wasn't there. It was fun whether we ended up playing a game or not.

So, when you want to collect up a few children, get a game of **All Aboard** going. Turn yourself into a train and make tracks through the playing area. Stop close to children who are alone or who seem to be looking for something to do, blow your whistle and chant: "This train is going out to the field to play _____"(dodge ball, tag, hide and seek or any other game). "All aboard who want to come aboard!" Steam through the playground with whoever wants to hook on and then get the promised game going.

I'LL BE YOUR PARTNER

Cat's Cradle And Other String Games

To play **Cat's Cradle** and other string games, you need a piece of string or yarn about four feet long tied in a loop. You also need two people (or a step by step book) to show everyone how to loop the string and lift it off each other's hands to make new patterns. Once the steps have been demonstrated, children divide into pairs with their own loop of string and learn to go through the routines. The demonstrators move from partner to partner helping out. Once partners have made a cat's cradle sequence with one partner, they find another partner to play with. If the string gets tangled, just start all over again.

Three-Legged Circus

Piggy-back tricks, three-legged races and partner acrobats are ways that ability differences can become a celebration of life. It doesn't matter who comes in first when the goal is simply for everyone to make it to the finish line in partners or small groups. Children change partners at the end of each challenge. Here are a few tricks to try.

- Walk from one end of the room to the other while balancing a beach ball between each other's shoulders.
- Run a three-legged race, a wheel barrow race or a piggy back race.
- Stand back to back and then sit down and stand up.
- Play leap frog.
- Help each other through an obstacle course.
- Create a hula hoop dance.
- Make numbers, letters or other shapes together.
- Lay down feet to feet and roll across the floor with toes touching.
- Get into partners and invent more circus tricks to perform for others.

Piggy-back tricks, three-legged races and partner acrobats are ways that ability differences can become a celebration of life.

I'LL BE YOUR PARTNER

Partner to Partner

In this fast moving game, the leader calls out "Partner to Partner!" in a loud commanding voice. This is the signal for everyone to sort themselves into two-way or three-way partnerships as quickly as possible. Once all the children are matched up with one or two other kids, the leader calls out instructions to link up in different ways. For example:

- back to back *(stand back to back)*
- toe to toe *(stand toe to toe)*
- hand to foot *(one person's hand on the other person's foot)*
- elbow to head *(one person's elbow on the other person's head)*

After calling out several instructions, someone becomes a new leader by calling out "Partner to Partner" in a loud commanding voice and everyone finds different partners.

Autograph Race

Each time a child is collecting an autograph from someone, he or she is experiencing being in partnership with that person.

Children of all ages seem to love filling out forms and exchanging autographs. Hand out a blank piece of paper and a pen to each person, and call out categories such as these examples.

- Find someone who loves swimming and get their autograph.
- Find someone who is an artist and get their autograph.
- Find someone who is older than you and get their autograph.

Each time a child is collecting an autograph from someone, he or she is experiencing being in partnership with that person.

- Instead of calling out categories, you can hand out a list and children can get into partners or small groups and go on an autograph scavenger hunt.
- A group can make up an autograph scavenger hunt on the spot. Simply brainstorm a list of people to find, post the list on a blackboard or flip chart and begin searching your group for those gifted people.

Connected Statues

Everyone finds one or two partners. Each partnership or small group selects a card with a picture or name of an animal or object on it. They connect together into a statue that shows that animal or object. Everyone else guesses what it is.

- Instead of picking a card, one set of children could go around and whisper an animal or object to each small group.
- This can be played as a circle game by batting three balloons up into the air. Whoever catches a balloon comes in the center. The children who are around the circle suggest a statue for the threesome to make. Once the three have created their statue, they bat the balloons up high in the air. The three children who catch them come in the middle to make another statue.

Jigsaw Puzzle Partners

Jigsaw puzzle games are great ways for kids to find partners or solve a puzzle in partners. There are many variations.

- **Puzzle Hunt:** Everyone gets into partners or small groups and finds pieces of a puzzle or a construction toy that are hidden around the room or an outdoor area. After they find them, they help each other put the pieces together.

- **Fruit Salad:** Each pair or small group finds one type of fruit (in the store or on the vine!) brings it back to cut up and put in a bowl to make a fruit salad.

- **Jigsaw Meal:** Each pair or small group prepares a part of a meal and then everyone shares it.

- **Natural Puzzles:** Each pair goes to a different area and identifies as many living beings as possible. After a set period of time, they come back to the main group and take turns making a master list of the things that only one group observed. This rule encourages everyone to notice the hidden aspects of the natural world.

- **Pieces of Art:** Make simple puzzles by cutting up photographs, drawings, sentences, riddles or art work into two or three pieces. You can also find toys and games that have two or three parts. Now that you have a bunch of small puzzles, hand a piece out to each person in the group. Once they find each other they will be in partners or small groups and ready for the next activity.

Duets

Children get into pairs or small groups and then take some time to create entertainment to perform for everyone else. This could be done on the spur of the moment as an improvisational drama activity or children could spend several minutes, hours or even days rehearsing. Some possible forms of entertainment are music, poems, dancing, clapping games, tricks, riddles, jokes and show and tell. Encourage performers to get the audience actively involved.

take some time to create entertainment to perform for everyone else.

Buddy Nature Walk

Get into partners and go for a walk in a natural area. A set of partners calls out something for the rest of the group to pay attention to. For example: "Pay attention to insects", "Notice the wind", "Look for reflections", "Find examples of erosion". After walking for a few moments, the lead partners stop and wait for the rest of the partners to catch up to each other, they get in a circle and take turns talking about what they have noticed. If the group wants to, they can divide into new partnerships and give someone else a turn to suggest what to observe.

GIVE AND TAKE

Maori Stick Dancing

FROM ALAN ARMSTRONG (1986)
**GAMES AND DANCES OF THE
MAORI PEOPLE**. NEW ZEALAND:
VIKING SEVENSEAS.
REPRINTED WITH PERMISSION.

A few days after John and I arrived in Micronesia, I complimented a young girl on her beautiful shell necklace. *"Wow, what a nice necklace!"* I said in my friendly way. I was mortified with guilt when she took it off and gave it to me! This was my introduction to a gift-giving culture where wealth is measured by how much people give away instead by how much they have saved. Despite my initial embarrassment, I came to love this way of living. People gave away much more than jewelry. The most common gifts were time and smiles. Saying hello without stopping to visit was unthinkable. Frowning or any other kind of negative communication were the most selfish acts possible.

At parties and meetings, people didn't converse back and forth like we were used to doing back home. Instead, children and adults took turns giving each other stories, jokes, action songs, dances and other entertainment. Throughout the week neighborhoods were filled with laughter and music because everyone was always practicing their gifts of song, music and dance that they would be giving away during feasts that took place almost every weekend. On Sundays, church services lasted several hours to make time for everyone's musical offerings.

One evening, without any preparation at all we found out that no one stays a spectator for long. An appreciative crowd hooted and laughed while John strummed the guitar and I sang "You Are My Sunshine" in sign language. The children's rhyme "Pease Porridge Hot, Pease Porridge Cold" was our desperate encore!

Over the months of living in this kind and caring culture, the problems of the world that used to concern me so much moved into the back of my mind and good times with people moved into the front. One morning when I was brushing my hair, I looked in the mirror and realized that the worry lines between my eyebrows had completely disappeared. Now back in Canada, my worry lines have returned over the years, but I find that I can recapture the joy of giving and giving whenever I take the time to connect with others through play.

Tis a gift to be simple, 'tis a gift to be free
Tis a gift to come down to where we ought to be
And when we find ourselves in the place just right
Twill be in the valley of love and delight

(SHAKER HYMN)

SKILL 6: GIVE AND TAKE

GIVE AND TAKE

Children are continuously exchanging objects, actions, ideas and information as they interact. Playing a board game, building a fort, playing catch or playing a game of twenty questions all share this back and forth interaction. Think about having a conversation. Giving a new idea or asking a question is like offering a gift. Responding to an idea or answering a question is like accepting the gift. Giving another idea or asking another question keeps a conversational gift-exchange going.

Children who know how to give and take are able to:

- offer a contribution to share
- accept what is offered back
- offer another contribution
- and so on in a long cycle of back and forth turns

Inclusive leaders are very accepting of the many different gifts children have to offer and are able to "pick up the ball" in order to meet the challenges of keeping back and forth interactions going.

Giving another idea or asking another question keeps a conversational gift-exchange going.

Tip: It is human nature for people to give back what they have been given. Smiles, acknowledgments and other ways of welcoming can become an endless cycle of positive feedback that can multiply from one person to many others.

Here are several games and activities that give children enjoyable opportunities to practice give and take. Giving away the lead to others encourages everyone to develop their inclusive leadership skills.

Group Juggling Acts

Everyone stands in a circle. The leader who has lots of soft balls in a sack, makes eye contact with someone, says their name and carefully tosses them a ball in a way that they can catch it. (As in any game, it is just fine to ask "What is your name?" if you can't remember.) Once one ball has gone back and forth a few times, the leader adds in another ball and then another as the juggling begins to flow. If someone drops a ball, the leader quietly takes one ball out of play until the group seems ready for the challenge of another ball again. As everyone develops the skill of give and take, the group will be able to juggle more and more balls. You can play this game in many ways.

- Throw small soft balls or stuffed animals, large beach balls or balloons.

- Roll the balls to each other across a table or sitting on the floor.

- Stand together in partners and help each other throw balls to other partners and catch balls thrown by other partners.

- Leave out the name exchange and focus on making eye contact with each other before throwing the ball.

- Give every second child a ball. They throw the ball back and forth to a partner on the other side of the group. After throwing the ball back and forth a few times, stop the action, help everyone shift to a new partner and toss the balls back and forth again.

- Play a zig zag game in which each person always catches a ball thrown by the same person and throws the ball to another person. (Ted throws to Chandra who throws to Carmen who throws to Martin and so on.)

If the group can get a lot of balls going without dropping them, you are all ready to join the circus and perform under the big top!

Ask-Answer-Ask

Having a conversation is like playing catch.

Ask-Answer-Ask is best played in pairs or in a small circle of up to about five people. Start out with a light ball such as a nerf ball, a beach ball or a child's rubber ball and say, "Having a conversation is like playing catch. First you ask someone a question. This is like throwing the ball. Then, you answer the question. This is like catching the ball. Then you ask another question which is like throwing the ball again. If you aim carefully, throw well, catch quickly and then throw the ball again, you can keep the conversation going for a long time and you can help everyone take part."

Call someone's name and, once they are ready to receive, toss the ball to them while asking a small talk question such as these examples.

- "What did you think about the ball game last night?"

- "What did you do on the weekend?"

- "What's your favorite color?"

After the person catches the ball and answers the question, they can ask a question back or call out someone else's name and ask them a question. As the ball is being tossed back and forth from person to person the children are learning to have a conversation.

GIVE AND TAKE

CROSS-OVER GAMES

Cross-Over games are informal team games that help children practice the skill of give and take and get lots of exercise at the same time.

- **Cross-Over Dodge Ball:** The object of Cross-Over Dodge Ball is to get everyone onto the same side. Gather up lots of soft rubber balls (about one ball for every two or three children). Draw a line or lay a skipping rope down to split the field in half. Using an under-hand throw to keep the balls low, the children throw soft rubber balls back and forth. If someone catches the ball, they throw it back to the other side. If someone gets hit by the ball below the waist they cross over to the other side. When everyone is on the same side then everyone wins!

- **Giants, Wizards, Goblins** is an active version of the **Scissors, Paper, Rock** game that children play with their hands (see page 48). Everyone gets into two groups. The groups move apart from each other and secretly decide if they will be Giants (stand on tiptoes and raise arms), Wizards (cast a spell) or Goblins (crouch down). Then they move toward each other acting out their parts as they chant three times. "Giants, Wizards, Goblins; Giants, Wizards, Goblins; Giants, Wizards, Goblins" Then they say "We are _____" and simultaneously act out if they are Giants, Wizards or Goblins. Giants step on Wizards, Wizards put spells on Goblins, and Goblins run under Giants' legs.

  If both groups have selected the same magical being, it is a tie and they move apart and decide all over again. If each group has selected a different being, the members of the temporarily superior group chase and try to tag the other team members before they make it back to their safe area. Tagged members join the other team.

  Play until everyone is on one side or has melted together into a laughing mixture of Giants, Wizards and Goblins!

- **Red Rover Soccer:** This is just as much fun and less dangerous than the traditional British game of **Red Rover**. Children get into two lines across the field from each other but within calling distance. They stand side by side with legs apart and each person's feet touching the foot of the person beside them. Everyone on one side says "Red Rover, Red Rover, we want _____ to come over". The person whose name is called comes up to the "kicking line" and tries to kick or underhand throw a soft rubber ball through everyone's legs. If the ball goes through, that person stays on the same side. If the ball bounces back or fouls by going above someone's waist, that person crosses over. Now the other side gets a turn to call one or two children to kick or throw a rubber ball over.

Play until everyone is on one side or has melted together into a laughing mixture.

GIVE AND TAKE

this game can easily be adapted to overcome literacy barriers by using pictures.

QUESTION AND ANSWER GAMES

Children can practice give and take for hours on end by playing question and answer games, as well as singing and reciting music, songs, jokes, riddles and poetry that go back and forth.

Jam Sessions with musical instruments are an example of back and forth music. Also see **Rhythm And Movement Jam Sessions** (page 87).

Ask Me About Me: This game gives children a chance to exchange information about their favorite topics. Give each child a name tag. Instead of writing down their name, they write down a topic they would like to be asked about. For example, one child could write down "Ask me about my family." Another child could write down "Ask me about my favourite sports." Children mingle, exchange names, take turns asking and answering a couple of questions about the topics on their name tags and then mingle some more.

This game can easily be adapted to overcome literacy barriers by using pictures. Instead of writing topics have each child wear a photograph or cut a picture out of a magazine that is related to a favorite topic.

Who Came Back: Children get into two groups to play this question and answer game.

    Group One: "Who came back?"
    Group Two: "_____ (famous person's name) came back."   *(all repeat)*
    Group One: "Where from?"
    Group Two: "From _____ (a place)."   *(all repeat)*
    Group One: "With what?"
    Group Two: "With _____ (an object)!"   *(all repeat)*

Repeat with Group 2 asking the questions and Group 1 giving the answers. The results of this simple back and forth game are hilarious.

The Why Game: This question and answer game never ends.

    "Why did you _____ (name an action)?" • "Because _____ (give a reason)."
    "Why did you _____ (repeat reason)?" • "Because _____ (give another reason)."
    "Why did you _____ (repeat reason)?" • "Because _____ (give another reason)."
    "Why did you _____ (repeat reason)?" • "Because _____ (give another reason)."
    "Why did you _____ (repeat reason)?" • "Because _____ (give another reason)."
    …and so on.

CARD GAMES

Playing cards is a great way to learn how to exchange gifts back and forth. Classic games such as Go Fish and Crazy Eights have winners and losers, but when children play in partners or play the same game again and again, everyone has a chance to win.

MULTi-CULTURAL GifT eXCHANGE

Beginning with the families of the children you are guiding to explore diversity, go on an expedition to explore gift-giving and gift-receiving traditions in your community and around the world. Here are a few ideas.

- Interview families to find out their customs for giving and receiving gifts.

- Ask families to tell stories about special occasions or special memories of gifts given and received.

- Watch or role-play gift-giving ceremonies from different cultures.

- Play a gift giving game from another country. The Easter Egg Hunt from Central Europe, the Mexican Piñata, Chinese Fortune Cookies and the Fishing Game from Irish country fairs are four gift giving games. There are many many more.

CReATive GifTs

Make up your own gift-giving ceremonies and games. Here are a few ideas.

- Organize pot luck gift exchanges where everyone recycles their treasures.

- Give out awards for everyone that were purchased from a second-hand store.

- Each child wraps a homemade gift in many layers of newspaper. Now, everyone gathers in a circle and the gift exchange begins. Children keep exchanging gifts and removing one layer of newspaper at a time, until each child has uncovered one surprise gift each. (Be sure to recycle the newspapers.)

Explore gift-giving and gift-receiving traditions in your community and around the world.

Jam sessions with musical instruments are an example of back and forth music.

GIVE AND TAKE

MY TURN, YOUR TURN STORYTELLING

Taking turns reading or telling stories a sentence or paragraph at a time is a wonderful way of exchanging the gift of literacy. Look for multi-cultural stories about giving and receiving gifts. Here are a few examples.

- *Something From Nothing* by Phoebe Gilman
- *Chicken Sunday* by Patricia Polacco
- *The Patchwork Quilt* by Valerie Flournoy
- *Sam and the Lucky Money* by Karen Chinn
- *The Goat in the Rug* by Charles Blood
- *The Bracelet* by Yoshiko Uchida
- *A Carp for Kimoko* by Katherine Roundtree
- *Tell Me Again About The Night I Was Born* by Jamie Lee Curtis

Make up your own stories about gifts given and received by adding ideas to these opening lines.

- "What could it be?" Yolande wondered as she stared at the unopened package.
- Vanessa opened the card first and read, "This gift used to belong to your Grandmother."
- Kirsten answered the phone. A strange voice said "Your wish has been granted," and then hung up.
- As the big day drew closer, Hazura began to panic. What could he possibly give on such a great occasion?
- Make up your own opening lines for stories about giving and receiving.

Ask each other these questions and then make up a story that contains your answers.

- "Who are the main characters?"
- "What resources do they have with them?"
- "Where does this story take place?"
- "What has happened just before the story starts?"

Also see **Add-on Story Telling** (page 104) for more ideas.

Make up your own stories about gifts given and received.

ONCE UPON A TIME . . .

DECORATING CUPCAKES

GIVE AND TAKE

Give each child a cupcake (or a plain cookie or ice cream) and one type of icing, sprinkles, chocolate chips, raisins or other decoration. Children exchange decorations while making their cupcakes into beautiful creations. What else can children take turns decorating?

- A few edible ideas are Dried Fruit and Popcorn Necklaces, Shish-Ka-Bobs, Easter Eggs and Gingerbread Houses.
- A few inedible ideas are Greeting Cards, Pet Rocks and Homemade Boats.

COOPERATIVE POTTERY

In this artistic game for pairs or a small group, each person begins with a lump of play dough or clay. The goal is for each person to make a work of art. The rule is to make two of each part and then exchange one of them with someone else. For example, someone might make two balls and exchange one of them for a rolled coil and so on. It is amazing how, even though each sculptor has the same materials and shapes, each sculpture will turn out somewhat different.

TREASURES FROM NATURE

Gather up a collection of natural treasures such as shells, rocks, feathers, pine cones and hide them in a box. With eyes closed, a child reaches into the box, selects a treasure and holds it behind her back. Now that the object is hidden, she can open her eyes. The other children take turns asking the child questions about her object. Here are some types of questions to ask.

- What color do you think your treasure is?
- How old do you think your treasure is?
- Where do you think your treasure came from?
- What animals or plants do you think value your treasure?
- What do you think your treasure is?

After a few guesses, the child gets to look at her treasure and then everyone can share their natural knowledge about that object.

BIRD WATCHING

there are expert birders in almost every community who would enjoy the chance to help kids connect with nature.

Going outside together with binoculars and a bird book to help each other identify birds is a great way of practicing the skill of give and take. Children will be passing the binoculars back and forth, telling each other what they notice and figuring out what kind of "little brown bird" that might be. If you don't know anything about birds yourself, birding is a very popular hobby and there are expert birders in almost every community who would enjoy the chance to help kids connect with nature. You could also go outside together to identify insects, flowers, marine life or any part of our beautiful natural world.

TOUCH CONTROL AND OTHER SAFETY SKILLS

Kevin shares, *"When I was in school my baby daughter Kira attended the Growing Together Day Care Center, and I was involved in their Young Parents Program. One afternoon I attended a workshop about learning through play. I was the only guy who showed up so that made me a bit uncomfortable, but the other thing was that the idea of playing with my baby scared me a bit. Showing affection was difficult for me because of the way I was brought up. Push always came to shove when my brothers and I played. If one of us had a toy, the other would grab it whether he wanted it or not. We used to be really rough with each other and I didn't want my girl growing up like that."*

Self Portrait by kevin

Kevin's strong love for his child and his motivation to become a gentle influence won out over his initial apprehension. This tattooed graduate from the school of hard knocks allowed his innocence to emerge into the foreground of his life for a couple of hours. He became more and more enthusiastic as he participated in **Patty Cake, Patty Cake** (page 63), **Chain Reaction** (page 62) and **Doctor Dodge Ball** (page 98). He even built up enough trust in everyone to agree to take a turn being lifted up in a blanket and carried around the room. Before our eyes, he made a dramatic shift from struggling to control his anger over the way his life had been, to developing his gentle artistic nature.

He concludes, *"It was quite a turning point. Just after learning all these experiences, I wanted to share them right away so I went out and tried to find where I could go to teach people about sharing and all that. For the rest of the year, I volunteered on Friday and Saturday nights at the Youth Center. I loved it because the age of the kids went from about seven right up to over twenty. We played **Dodge Ball** and those other games, and I organized dances too. Now, Kira just had her second birthday and she still loves playing **Patty Cake** with me."*

(KEVIN SHIELL)

"Ice Skating" by Sayna, age 9

Bruce was a popular captain of his soccer team who loved to win more than anything and had never thought much about the kids he dismissed as "losers". After a few weeks of exploring cooperative games he was more understanding. *"You can still play just as fast and have as much fun in a friendly game of soccer or basketball without playing so rough. It's basically just being careful and not hitting. Like, if you want to say something to someone, you just tap them. You don't go up and hit them because sometimes that hurts people. You respect the other kids and you will be respected back. Then if you go up to a person and they say 'Hi' to you and you end up saying 'Hi' back and just waving then you end up being nice. If you are nice, they will be nice to you."*

SKILL 7: TOUCH CONTROL AND OTHER SAFETY SKILLS

TOUCH
CONTROL AND
OTHER
SAFETY SKILLS

Watch any skilled athlete and you will see touch control in action. Skiers learn to hurtle down steep slopes without crashing into other people, the trees or any other obstacles. Basketball players can handle a ball so skillfully that it looks like a dance. Together the horse and rider jump high walls in perfect unison. Figure skaters and acrobats support each other to leap, balance and spin in ways that seem effortless to those of us watching. Some everyday examples of touch control are shaking hands considerately, and lining up without pushing. Respecting privacy and personal boundaries are also forms of touch control.

Children begin learning touch control from early childhood onwards. Miss Sharrock, my Sixth Grade teacher used to tell us over and over again: *"Your freedom ends where another's begins."* Children who have good touch control are able to interact with each other safely even in crowded places and even when playing fast-paced, high energy sports such as karate or soccer. They know when and how to touch without being rough or otherwise making others feel uncomfortable or unsafe.

Your freedom ends where another's begins.

They can also show touch control by:

- tagging a person on the shoulder without hitting so hard that it hurts

- holding hands in a game without twisting someone's arm

- grabbing the ball in a game of basketball without grabbing the person along with it

- supporting someone to balance without pulling or pushing

When everyone in a group shares responsibility for touch control, then everyone feels safe to participate in more and more challenging games and activities.

Tip: Inclusive leaders review and demonstrate the rules for touch control before any new game or challenging activity and to any children who are new to the group. Then they stand by, ready to give kids a hand or an off-stage prompt if needed, until everyone is using touch control automatically.

TOUCH CONTROL AND OTHER SAFETY SKILLS

Here are games and activities that give children enjoyable opportunities to develop and practice touch control.

May We Come Closer?

This variation on the traditional game of **Mother May I?** gives children practice in establishing and maintaining physical boundaries. One child stands in the middle of a large open space and the other children scatter. Everyone calls out together: "May We Come Closer?" The child in the middle says "Yes, you may take (number) (type of steps) closer." or "No, you may take (number) (type of steps) away from me." Some popular types of movements are giant steps, side steps, baby steps, backward jumps, one-legged hops, tip toes and duck waddles. After the children comply, they say "May We Come Closer?" again. The back and forth process continues until the child in the middle answers "You are all just right." Now the circle scatters again and everyone follows another child's instructions until they are gathered around in a way that feels just right to that child.

Touch Control Challenge

Make up flash cards with various touch control challenges on them.

Make up flash cards with various touch control challenges on them, add in a board game such as Parcheesi, Trivial Pursuit, or Snakes and Ladders and you are ready to play **Touch Control Challenge**. A turn has these steps.

- The child who is taking a turn partners with whoever is currently in last place on the board.
- They pick a challenge card and perform the touch control challenge.
- They shake the dice and each move the number of spaces rolled.

Some possible touch control challenges are:
- give a high five
- show how you stand side by side in a crowded elevator,
- demonstrate a clapping game
- thumb wrestle politely
- congratulate each other for winning a race
- show how you shake on a promise
- tap each other on the shoulder
- help each other do a head stand
- support each other to stand on one foot and count backwards from ten to one

Chain Reaction

Everyone stands in a circle. The leader passes a touch on to the person on one side or the other side. The touch could be a secret handshake, a high five, a tap on the shoulder, an elbow nudge or some other example of touch control. Each person passes the touch on in a chain reaction until it gets back to the beginning again. Once a touch makes it around the circle once, you can increase the challenge by passing a series of two or more touches around the circle or you can get chain reactions going in both directions.

Shrinking Islands

This is a game that works best as a review game with a group of children who are already skilled at respectful touch control. This game is played somewhat like musical chairs, except when the music stops the island shrinks. (A chair, cushion or a piece of carpet is pulled away or the area marked out with rope is made smaller.) The objective is to safely get all the kids to fit on fewer and fewer or smaller and smaller islands.

Color Coded Musical Chairs

Set up chairs and color code them with tape, ribbon, wool or colored paper. When the music starts the children march around the chairs. When the music stops, call out a color. The goal is for every child to touch a chair that goes with that color. Once that is accomplished, remove a chair and start the music. By the end of the game everyone is crowded around and onto a single chair.

Lifts And Carries

Learning to carry each other safely is another great way to develop touch control.

- Two people of about the same height can link arms to make a sturdy seat and carry a third person from one place to another.

- An entire group can work together to help each other safely lift a person up. Once airborne, the volunteer can be carried from one place to another or passed from pair to pair along a double line. As trust builds, the group can try variations such as being lifted in a blanket or being lifted with eyes closed.

- Once the group can lift and carry safely, a narrator can tell a story about sailing across the ocean, flying a plane to another country or riding on an elephant while the group lifts and carries a volunteer in ways that match the words.

Tricks And Stunts

Exchange Clapping Poems, Secret Handshakes, Juggling Tricks, Gymnastics, Dance Steps and more complicated sequences of movements and stunts that you have learned with each other. Also see **Three-Legged Circus** (page 49), **Video Feedback** (page 94) and **Spot Dance Challenge** (page 136).

- Children pick up many interesting moves from relatives, friends, participation in sports and clubs and from television. If the appropriate safety precautions are taken and the moves are taught one at a time at a slow pace, children can also enjoyably learn many more complicated tricks and stunts.

- Ask a recreation leader, physical education teacher, coach or instructor to demonstrate some routines and pass on the basic safety rules of checking out the physical space, spotting each other, learning a move one step at a time and other precautions to prevent accidents.

- **Patty Cake, Patty Cake** is a simple clapping poem. Any pre-school teacher can teach you many more.

TOUCH CONTROL AND OTHER SAFETY SKILLS

Learning to carry each other safely is another great way to develop touch control.

TOUCH CONTROL AND OTHER SAFETY SKILLS

Children who are educated about what they see on television and skilled at fake fighting will be less likely to injure each other as they play.

Stage Effects And Trick Photography

Children benefit from learning to distinguish between stunts that are safe to learn through play, dangerous stunts that can only be done by professionals who have developed high levels of touch control, and stunts that can only be done with cameras or computers.

- Ask people involved in film, stage and wrestling to demonstrate how fighting scenes are staged and choreographed in ways that people almost never hurt each other and mostly don't even touch each other.

- Ask a photographer, film maker or videographer to show children the different ways that movies trick the eye.

- Make and edit videos of simple stunts, including fake fighting scenes.

Children who are educated about what they see on television and skilled at fake fighting will be less likely to injure each other as they play.

Touch Around The World

One of the tensions in diverse societies is that rules about touch vary around the world. People from different cultures, religions and lifestyles show wide variations in the dos and don'ts of greeting, playing, disciplining, helping, showing affection and showing intimacy. Going on a respectful exploration of these different rules and values, without trying to change each other, can help children be more understanding and patient with differences in touch and body language. Invite children and their parents to explain and demonstrate the rules about touch from their family and from other cultures, religions and lifestyles that they are familiar with. Compare and contrast similarities and differences in:

- greeting each other

- getting each other's attention

- encouraging others

- disciplining others

- standing or sitting together

- showing affection

- showing respect

- showing aggression

- sharing food

- helping each other

- playing together

- showing intimacy

Explore differences within cultures and lifestyles depending on age, gender, status and type of relationship.

face Painting

Children develop touch control by learning how to do face painting and removable tattooing. Be sure to use washable, non-toxic paints and crayons. Encourage kids to try out designs on paper and on the backs of each other's hands first. Gradually build up trust to paint and color designs on each other's faces, arms and ankles. Learning to respect individual differences in preference for different kinds of designs and for physical boundaries is an important and essential part of developing touch control. Build awareness that different cultures and different individuals vary in what types of designs are considered to be attractive.

— TOUCH —
CONTROL AND
OTHER
SAFETY SKILLS

making Pizza

Working together in small groups or partners to spread a ball of pizza dough out into a flat crust is a motivating way to develop touch control. Washing hands first helps children be more aware of safety. Deciding on toppings teaches respect for choice, sharing and many other connecting skills. Waiting for a pizza to cook teaches patience. Eating homemade creations makes lunch and supper a lot more fun.

All Creatures Great And Small

Getting children involved in caring for animals, plants and the earth develops touch control and respect for all living beings. There are opportunities to care for living beings in every community around the world.

Getting children involved in caring for animals, plants and the earth develops touch control and respect for all living beings.

- At home, children can care for pets, grow flowers and vegetables indoors or outdoors, or watch out for a birds nest or a wild-life tree.

- In their neighborhoods, children can get to know and help look after local pets, gardens and wild areas. They can also arrange to take their dog or cat over to visit elderly people in the community.

- Children can volunteer at organizations in the community that care about animals, plants and the earth. Some examples are conservation and environmental groups, farming organizations such as 4-H Clubs, hiking clubs, organizations that protect animals, "adopt a highway" and "adopt a beach" clean-up projects. Also see **Conservation And Land Stewardship** (page 143).

DARING TO BE DIFFERENT

BLACK LIKE ME

I often felt bad
When people called me:
    'Black like the charcoal
    And dark as the night'
To expound their ignorance.

I often felt insulted
When people whispered about me:
    'Black like the tar
    And dark as the coal'
To prescribe   their pride.

But I felt honoured.
When people greeted me:
    'Black like darkness
    And dark as blackness'
To describe my identity.

Say "Black like me!"
Sing "Black is beautiful!"
Shout "Black is powerful!"
    "Whoever is not proud
    of his own colour is
    not fit to live"

In the beginning, God
Created us out of darkness.
For without darkness
There is no lightness
And without blackness
There is no whiteness.

FROM ALFRED GHERE LILEGETO (1984) **WE, THE VILLAGERS**.
SOLOMON ISLANDS: UNIVERSITY OF THE SOUTH PACIFIC.
REPRINTED HERE WITH PERMISSION.

by Daniel Mason, age 16

by Natalie Donahue, age 15

DANIEL!

    A very different
    very creative
    very dramatic
    very sarcastic
    individual
    just like me!

DARE TO BE DIFFERENT

Hi
Daniel

NATALIE!

She is her
her so shy
Shy's not bad
with wings she flys.
Above, below, within
the rage
She's at her peak
When she's on stage

Drama's fun
fun she loves
Drawing flowers
hearts and doves
eskimos all short or tall
differences I loves them
all.

SKILL 8: DARING TO BE DIFFERENT

The keys to celebrating differences are being able to accept one's own differences and being able to understand each other's differences. Daring to be different means:

- being friendly and relaxed about your own and others' unique qualities

- feeling comfortable about standing out in appearance, culture, religion, color, age, disability or family background

- showing off languages you speak, talents you have, food you know how to cook and other skills you have learned

- educating yourself and others about your differences by showing or telling other people about anything they need to do differently in order to make a better connection

- opening your ears, eyes, minds and hearts to listen to other people's differences

- asking questions that are polite and show a positive interest that is genuine and not patronizing

- reaching out in welcome, giving a hand if needed and being ready to learn or invent new possibilities for making positive connections

Daring to be different means educating yourself and others about your differences.

 Caution: Children who are not used to being welcoming are likely to go back to habits of rejecting when inclusive leaders are not there. Children need time and support to build trusting connections before they will feel safe and respected enough to freely share their differences.

DARING
TO BE
DIFFERENT

We are looking
for someone
who can make a
difference!

Here are cooperative games and creative activities that give children interesting opportunities to celebrate their differences.

I Can Make A Difference!

This is an enjoyable cross-over game that begins with two groups standing in two lines facing each other. The first group calls out "We are looking for someone who can make a difference!"

Someone in the second group volunteers to go across, saying "I can make a difference by (name a talent, skill, action, idea or other difference)." For example, "I can make a difference by counting to 10 in Tagalog."

The first group says "Great, show us as you come across!" The volunteer demonstrates their difference and runs across to the other group. Now, it is the second group's turn to call out "We are looking for someone who can make a difference!"

Very Important People

Gather in a circle around a box with various props, hats and other costume accessories. Each child takes a turn coming into the middle of the circle. In unison, everyone says "_____ (name) we know you are a VIP (Very Important Person) who DARES to be different and unique. Tell or show us how!" With the help of a prop or two the child shows and tells about a difference (also see **Self Defense**, page 131).

Finding Out What We Don't Have In Common

Help each child find a partner or small group of children who they don't yet know very well. They interview each other and find out three things they do not have in common. Then they gather into a larger group and share the differences they have found.

- "Seth has three brothers and I have one sister."
- "I like reading, Trin likes art."
- "I have cerebral palsy and Julianne is the fastest runner in the school."
- "I just moved here and Surinder has lived here for his whole life."

Through The Years

Divide into partners or small groups and ask each other a few of these questions. Listen to each other's stories in response to each question.

- What is something different about your ancestors?
- What is something different about the story of your birth?
- What is something different about your first year of life?
- What is something different about your fifth year of life?
- What is something different about your tenth year of life?

  …and so on.

DARING
TO BE
DIFFERENT

Share one or more stories with the larger group. Here is a story that nine-year-old Katia Armstrong shared with her class:

A long, long, long, long time ago in the 1700s when my great, great, great, great grandmother was a little girl, she lived on the West Coast of Africa.

My great, great, great, great grandmother and her family had to walk many miles to slave forts on the Western Coast of Africa and then they were piled into slave ships and crossed the ocean. After many weeks they arrived in Haiti (where I was born). Many of the shipmates were sick, all were very tired and some had even died.

When my great, great, great, great grandmother arrived in Haiti, slave traders sold her and her family to plantation owners. This meant she was separated from her family (this was her mother, father and her siblings). She was sent work on a sugar plantation where she was treated very badly.

The language that my great, great, great, great grandmother spoke was Niger-Kordofanian. This made it difficult for her to communicate with the French plantation owners and some of the other slaves (from other parts of Africa) because they spoke different languages. This made it hard for her to understand what her master was saying to her. One day her master got mad, thinking she was ignoring him and he whipped her and whipped her till she thought she was going to die.

Sometimes late at night my great, great, great, great grandmother would tell the other slaves folk tales that her mother used to tell her when they were living in Africa. Telling folk tales and myths were a big part to the African culture and other slaves would often tell each other stories that they had also been told in Africa.

I really think that I'm very special to have a cool great, great, great, great grandmother. I think that I am special because I am related to her and she lived through life as slave. I really admire her because she was courageous and a very special woman.

A Different Sort Of Scavenger Hunt

Search your library for books and videos that celebrate differences. There are many resources about different languages, games, creative activities, people and natural wonders in our interconnected world. There are many books and videos for children who are exploring diversity.

there are many books and videos for children who are exploring diversity.

🖎 Here are a few of many thousands of book titles to get you started:

Glasses, Who Needs Em? by Lane Smith
Frederick by Leo Lionni
Is Your Family Like Mine? by Lois Abrumchik
One Dad, Two Dads by Johnny Valentine
Jamaica Tag-Along by Juanita Havill
Silver Wings by Kenneth Oppel
A Promise is a Promise by Robert Munsch

🖎 These are a few of many video titles available from National Film Board of Canada:

I'll Find A Way
Just A Wedding
Pictures Out Of My Life
Under The Rainbow
Kazuby

Don't forget that the most important parts of reading books or watching videos are the discussions and explorations that follow.

DARING
TO BE
DIFFERENT

Toys And Treasures

Sharing childhood toys and family treasures helps children to understand different values, including the value that the most inclusive things in life are free. Children can also share information about toys and treasures through art, stories, and other creative ways of communicating. Some toys and treasures children might share with each other include:

- collections of stamps, rocks, cards, dolls, ornaments and music
- home-made games and toys
- traditional toys from the attic such as yo-yos, jacks, balls, spinning tops and skipping ropes
- souvenirs of special times
- family heirlooms and special gifts

Toys and treasures do not need to cost money. Handmade playthings, recycled toys, and natural treasures are very valuable because of the ingenuity, time, learning and love that have been put in to them.

And Now For Something Completely Different

In a welcoming group, children become more and more comfortable with showing off their differences as gifts. Give children opportunities to dare to educate each other about their differences by leading activities that explore those differences.

Children could:

- give a demonstration of how to do something different
- lead songs, dances, games or other activities
- show photographs, maps or pictures from magazines
- tell about a unique experience or explain about something different they enjoy doing
- take everyone to an interesting place
- bring an interesting visitor

The world has no limit when children dare share their differences together!

In a welcoming group, children become more and more comfortable with showing off their differences as gifts.

My Very Different Day

Guide children to draw cartoon strips showing the many different ways various people they know live their everyday lives. A friend who uses a wheelchair once commented, "I do everything that you do. What is really different is how I get those things done." Encourage each child to get beyond stereotypes by thinking about themselves, their family members and other real people doing real things such as:

- waking up, dressing, eating, bathing and going to bed
- cooking, cleaning, gardening and other chores around home
- going out to school, play, work, a store or a place of worship
- doing things with family, friends and other people

Making A Difference Portrait Gallery

Help each other draw self portraits. There are many ways to draw pictures of each other. Children could:

- trace each other's shadows, profiles or entire bodies and then draw in hair, eyes, mouths, clothing and other features
- enlarge photographs of each other or the group on a photocopy machine
- draw caricatures that positively exaggerate each person's unique qualities
- make sculptures out of play dough or modeling clay
- make masks out of papier maché
- paint self portraits on balloons

Next, visit each other's portraits in partners or small groups and draw or write positive messages that acknowledge and value each person's different and unique qualities. Present the resulting portraits to each other in a ceremony that emphasizes how important each person is.

Draw or write positive messages that acknowledge and value each person's different and unique qualities.

Different Ways Of Eating

Explore the many different customs, habits and strategies for eating and sharing food.

- Invite parents to help children demonstrate how meals are prepared, served and eaten at home.
- Bring in different eating utensils and compare customs and strategies for eating soup, spaghetti, sushi and other foods.
- Learn about food rules related to customs, religions, family preferences, health, allergies and personal decisions.
- Learn about table manners in different homes and in different settings.
- Learn how to respectfully serve food to people who live with various ability differences. Some examples are blindness, wearing braces, mobility differences, being very young or very old.

Biodiversity

Explore diversity in nature by learning about different eco-systems such as inter-tidal zones, marshes, mud-flats, mountains, ponds, swamps, rivers or deserts. Find out how all the different climates, plants, animals, rocks, water and weather systems are part of interconnected webs of life. You could:

- visit a marine laboratory
- go out in the field with a biologist or naturalist
- go out yourselves to look inside a hollow log or under a rock

Exploring eco-systems has the same precautions as the science fiction movies that warn about the dangers of time travel. Be careful to look without disturbing the living beings you are visiting. Soon children will be appreciating many, many different living beings and relationships they were never aware of before.

FOLLOWING THE LEADERS BEHIND YOU

In a group of students from several different countries who were all learning English the students from Europe were very talkative, while the students from the countries around the Pacific Rim were mostly silent. To try to shift things a bit we played a variation on the game called **Back to Front** (see page 76). First we pulled a topic out of a hat. It was something about the pros and cons of zoos and wildlife reserves. Then, we began the discussion. Sonja, Greta, and Jennifer leaped into the discussion quickly. They each made many interesting points about the importance of zoos and reserves for educating children, the need to protect endangered species, and the problems of poaching in National Parks. After five minutes, I called "Time!" and froze the action. Acknowledging the depth of the discussion so far, I asked these three young women, who had given so many contributions, to put their own ideas on hold and shift into practicing the silent discussion skills of paying attention, making eye contact, nodding and smiling. At the same time, I asked the group members who were already proficient at giving silent background support to push themselves to make more active contributions. During the next five minutes Anita, Adriana, and Felicia quickly entered the spotlight and talked at length about points ranging from the beauty of a well-designed zoo to concerns about destruction of wild life habitats in Indonesia, to the effects of wildlife reserves on local eco-systems. Sonja, Greta and Jennifer were astonished at how much they had to say. *"We didn't even know you could speak English so well! Why haven't you ever spoken up before?"* Jenny asked. Anita and Felicia laughed a bit while Adriana explained, *"In our Filipino culture it is very impolite to interrupt, so we have been waiting for our turn."*

Outdoor educator, Michael Cohen tells this story of a leader who came out from behind the scenes during his elementary school graduation:

"As the ceremony concluded, amongst the students a chant spontaneously arose and grew 'We want Minny! We want Minny!' It would not cease, but became louder and embarrassed the school staff who hushed us to no avail… Minny was the quiet cleaning woman, the small gentle bent white haired lady who pushed the mop and broom through the halls every day and washed the blackboards. Officials never thought to include her in our good-bye ceremony. Their work, not hers, was what education was all about. For 20 minutes, as the chanting continued, administrators searched the halls and classrooms for Minny. They finally located her… Shy halting, almost against her will, they brought Minny to the stage in her simple blue and white, slightly soiled work uniform. We went wild! Our roar of approval put to shame our applause for our teachers. The underdog had its day."

FROM MICHAEL J. COHEN (1997) **WELL MIND, WELL EARTH.**
WASHINGTON: WORLD PEACE UNIVERSITY PRESS.
REPRINTED HERE WITH PERMISSION.

Everyone who has run down the street to catch up to a galloping two year old has had the experience of following a leader behind them.
Did you pick him up and carry him back to the rest of the group or did you fall under the spell of this miniature pied piper and follow his lead even for a few moments?

Quaker cartoon

SKILL 9: FOLLOWING THE LEADERS BEHIND YOU

FOLLOWING THE LEADERS BEHIND YOU

Inclusive leaders do not fall for the common assumptions that the kids in the back are not capable or don't want to get involved. Inclusive leaders don't cover their ears when they hear the beat of a different drummer. They don't duck when ideas pop up out of left field. Inclusive travel guides remember to look for and encourage leadership from the people behind the scenes as well as from the obvious leaders who are in the front and center of the action. Following the leaders behind you without losing sight of safety, equality, choice and fun can lead a group to interesting and completely unexpected discoveries.

Following the leaders behind you involves paying more attention to the people in the group than to the task at hand.

Following the leaders behind you without losing sight of safety, equality, choice and fun can lead a group to interesting and completely unexpected discoveries.

 Offer a turn to the person standing quietly.

 Turn to people on the edges of a group and ask for their observations and ideas.

 Incorporate suggestions that are different than what you had in mind.

 Talk to quiet children during quiet times when they are more likely to feel comfortable about giving ideas.

 Respond to children's body language and gestures as well as to their words.

 Open communication up by taking steps to understand people who are fluent in different languages than you are. Interpreters can help bridge language differences.

The people in the back have a very different view of what is going on and have a much wider viewpoint than the close-up focus in the center of the action. This is why they have such potential to shift everyone to view things in completely new ways.

 Caution: Throughout history, people have been forced to hide their leadership potential because of fears of rejection and censure. The inclusive ground rules of safety, equality, choice and fun are essential for everyone to be able to share leadership without fear of backlash or other negative repercussions.

Here are several games, activities and experiences that give children a chance to practice following the leaders behind them.

Catch The dragon's Tail

Children get in a line, one person behind the other and hold on to each other by the waist. The front person is the fiery head of the dragon. The last person (the leader at the back of the group) is the tail.

The goal is for the head of the dragon to catch its own tail end. This means that the tail of the dragon is actually leading the chase around the room by twisting, dodging and otherwise eluding the head of the dragon.

When the head finally catches the tail, the second child lets go of the head's waist and instantly transforms into the new head of the dragon while the child who was the head becomes the tail.

The new head of the dragon draws a fiery breath or two to give the new tail a chance to get ready to lead another chase around the room, going this way and that way to avoid getting tagged for as long as possible.

Mouse Trap

Being outside of the inner circle is the goal in this silly strategy game. Make about a third of the group into mice who stay outside the circular trap formed by everyone else holding hands.

The mice circle around the trap waiting for a chance to get at the imaginary cheese in the center. The children in the circle chant, "Mouse, mouse, mouse, mouse…"

Eventually someone calls out "Set the mouse trap" and everyone raises their hands. Now the mice weave in and out of the children's hands, being careful not to be in the trap too long, but being daring enough to go in long enough to nibble at that delicious cheese.

Sooner or later, someone calls out "Snap!" and everyone snaps their hands down.

The mice on the outside of the circle have shown their cunning leadership by avoiding that trap and so they get to be mice again. The mice on the inside trade with children in the circle and help set another trap.

Wink

A quiet, background style of leadership is often the most effective strategy in this suspenseful game. Go up to each child in turn and pretend to whisper and/or show them a signal.

A quiet, background style of leadership is often the most effective strategy.

Only one child actually receives the secret signal which is "WINK". The winker is the secret leader. His or her challenge is to go around the room and subtly cast spells on the other children by winking at them.

Any child who gets winked at sinks to the ground in a coma (sinking to the ground as dramatically as possible adds to the suspense). The goal is to discover the winker before being winked at! Children need to be careful though because anyone who makes a mistaken identification also falls into a coma.

When the winker is discovered, everyone wakes up and the child who discovered the winker gets to help with the job of carefully passing the "WINK" signal on to another secret leader. The suspense starts to build all over again. A few variations are:

🐑 select more than one winker

🐑 play the game in partners

🐑 play wearing masks

Sociometry

Give everyone opportunities to show their leadership non-verbally by asking children to measure their differences. You could ask children to sort themselves according to almost any dimension. Here are a few examples.

🐑 Ask children to measure how much activity they prefer. Children who prefer very quiet activities such as reading and drawing go in the middle. Children who prefer very noisy activities such as yelling and cheering, go out to the edges of the group.

🐑 Children could show long they have lived in the neighborhood (attended this school, come to this camp). A short time goes in the middle and a long time at the edges of the circle.

🐑 Ask children how close they live to _____ (name of a child or place). Close goes in the middle and far away stretches out toward the edges.

🐑 Ask about knowledge of a certain activity. Lots of knowledge goes in the middle and less knowledge around the edges.

After each sorting, ask children how they can help and get help from each other now that they are more aware of each other's differences. For example the children might decide that:

🐑 those who like to read have a lot of stories to tell

🐑 those who have been in this group a long time can show the newer members around

🐑 those who have a lot of knowledge about an area can guide the others to favorite places

Ask children how they can help and get help from each other now that they are more aware of each other's differences.

Partner Brainstorming

Before having a large group discussion, ask everyone to discuss the topic with the people beside them for a few moments. Then, when you have the discussion in the larger group, ask partners to help each other give ideas. This opens the door for children who are used to staying in the background to more comfortably put their ideas forward.

WHAT ARE YOUR IDEAS?

FOLLOWING THE LEADERS BEHIND YOU

Children who are quiet and reflective when they are the center of attention may prefer to show their leadership behind the scenes.

Back To Front

The challenge is to build a tall tower in the middle of the circle. This would be easy if only the children in the middle had the building equipment but they don't. They need to wait for the leaders who are in a circle around them to give them the resources and the instructions they need. To add to the challenge, add any of these rules.

- The leaders on the outside of the circle are the only ones who can talk.

- The leaders on the outside of the circle are the only ones who can see.

- The tower needs to be built before the timer goes off.

Instead of building a tower, children could make sandwiches, draw pictures, make a mosaic, build a boat, have a discussion or play a board game. Also see **From Our Point Of View** (page 82) and **Off-Stage Drawing** (page 105).

Who Am I?

Here is a game that gets children looking backwards because only the people behind them know who they are! Cut out pictures from magazines or write down names of well-known objects, plants, animals, people or characters from television, movies, books, cartoons and stories. (Get the kids to help.) Each child gets a picture pinned on his or her back and then asks people to look behind, and give clues or answer questions to help figure out what the picture is.

Masks, Puppets And Shadow Plays

Children who are quiet and reflective when they are the center of attention may prefer to show their leadership behind the scenes by giving their voice to a masked character, a puppet or a shadow actor. There are as many ways to make masks and puppets as there are ways to explore differences with them.

- Draw, paint, glue and cut faces on to pie plates. Then glue and sew hair and hats on to a stocking cap. Put on the cap, tie on the plate-face and enjoy the difference!

- Decorate a paper bag, cut out a place for eyes and try to figure out who that character is!

- Hang up a sheet, shine a light behind it and put on shadow plays.

- Draw a different character on each finger and you have a two-handed soap opera.

- Make puppets out of old socks, with buttons for eyes and wool for hair.

- Use dolls for puppets.

- Borrow puppets, masks and other costumes from a local drama group.

- Once everyone has a character or two, they can improvise, create plays or re-enact scripted plays.

🐿 Invite local actors, artists, entertainers and puppeteers to lead you on a creative adventure involving masks, puppets or shadow plays.

🐿 Go to the library and learn about puppets, masks and shadow figures from around the world and throughout history. Theatre has long been an important way for people from different backgrounds to educate others.

FOLLOWING THE LEADERS BEHIND YOU

Ancestors

Exchange memories about leaders and pioneers from past generations. A few of these leaders behind us are famous, but most are remembered more quietly by families who have saved stories and souvenirs that keep their memories alive. For example, my Grandmother never became famous and now she is only remembered by a few dozen people, but those of us who remember her know how much she taught us. We love to share our memories of her and to show off things she knit, furniture she brought with her from England, old photographs, as well as her stories she told about ancestors from previous generations.

Enrich your sharing by doing research. Attics, museums, archives, places of worship, cultural centers, veterans associations and historical societies are filled with memories of the leaders behind us. Take a look around your own community and see what you find. Libraries have many wonderful books and videos honoring well known and little known leaders from the past.

those of us who remember her know how much she taught us.

Where To Now?

This is a group walk in which the last child to arrive at each choice point gets a turn to tell the group where to go next. The group could take a short walk in the building or an all day hike that covers several miles.

Long Way Home

Go to a natural spot with a variety of trails and possible routes. Ask children to get into two groups. Children in the first group line up, one behind the other. Everyone except the front person blocks their vision by putting their heads down so they can only see the ground, keeping their eyes closed or wearing blindfolds. The children in the other group are spotters whose job is to make sure everyone is safe and to memorize the route. Or perhaps, one person could draw a map. The front person of the first group leads the followers on a complicated journey around trees and rocks, along different trails or crossing back and forth across the same trail. The children who have their eyes closed try to stay aware of where they are going by noticing the terrain, the smells, the sounds and by memorizing the twists and turns of the route. Every so often, the front person passes the leadership on to the next person in line, then goes to the end of the group, puts his or her head down and follows along. After every child has had a chance to lead, they open their eyes and try to retrace their route. The members of the second group call out "Stop" any time the first group goes off course as they are retracing the route. If needed, they can give clues to help the first group get back on track. Once the first group has retraced their route, it is the second group's turn to follow the leaders behind them and the first group's turn to make sure everyone is safe.

UNDERSTANDING IN ANY LANGUAGE

U R
2 niCE
2 B

4-GOTTEN

Rebus

I have learned a lot about understanding in any language from my friend Rosemarie who has been deaf since she was born. She is fluent in American Sign Language as well as English and she easily makes friends with people who speak different languages. Rosemarie also knows many musical languages. She is famous for her ability to interpret songs into ASL sign-dance and she performs Greek and Turkish dances with a multicultural folk-dance group. She tells me that her secret for unlocking all the languages of the world is to stay relaxed and listen patiently with her eyes and her heart to all kinds of communication. She never worries about figuring out accents or picking up every single word because she has developed the art of discerning the facial expressions, body language, eye movements, gestures, tones and rhythms that make up the language of the emotions behind words. Whenever I am with Rosemarie I feel completely and absolutely understood.

American Sign Language (ASL)

by Riley McIntosh, age 14

Braille

Practice thinking this...

It is OK not to understand every word.
I can understand lots with my eyes.
I have lots of time.
I can listen with my heart.
I am comfortable with ambiguity.

SKILL 10: UNDERSTANDING IN ANY LANGUAGE

**UNDERSTANDING
IN ANY
LANGUAGE**

The ability to reach across speech, language and communication differences with understanding is one of the foundations for building strong connections of respect, valuing and trust. If you can overcome feelings of embarrassment, frustration or impatience when communication is not easy, you can increase your skill at understanding all kinds of talking. You will be better able to understand different accents, dialects and languages and you will be better able to follow pointing, symbols, gestures, signing and pictures. The key is to feel comfortable about not understanding so that you can stay relaxed as you listen carefully with your eyes and your heart as well as your ears.

These steps will increase your ability to understand speech, language and other communication differences.

- Take extra time.

- Give your undivided attention to the person's words, facial expressions, gestures and body language.

- Relax yourself by focusing on your breathing and saying positive messages to yourself.

Stay relaxed as you listen carefully with your eyes and your heart as well as your ears.

- Listen actively by repeating back the "gist" of what you are picking up about the person's ideas and feelings:

- Accept and value support from fluent communicators, interpreters or any prepared information that is provided but at the same time, keep your focus on the person you are interacting with.

Caution: Remember not to guess, jump to conclusions or pretend that you understood; and be careful not to interrupt, take over the topic of conversation or ask more than one question at a time.

**UNDERSTANDING
IN ANY
LANGUAGE**

Here are several cooperative games, creative activities and outdoor experiences that give children enjoyable opportunities to practice understanding in any language.

Greetings Around The World

While learning each other's names, children can learn how to greet each other in many different languages. First go around the circle and ask each child to say hello in any language (include slang and gestures used by people of different ages and life styles). Then children go around the room greeting each other and teaching each other their different forms of greeting as well as their names. Back in the circle, go around the room once more and all together greet each child by their name in one or more of their languages.

*Fingerspelled
introductions*

You Speak My Language?

This is an enjoyable communication game for a large group of children. Make sets of flash cards showing about 5 pictures or words. (For example make 5 elephant cards, 5 lion cards, 5 parrot cards, 5 monkey cards and 5 snake cards for 25 children.) Hand out one flashcard to each child. Without showing the flashcards to each other, the children make the movements and sounds of the animal or object on their flash card. At the same time, they search for others who are making similar movements and sounds. Once everyone is gathered into small groups, they can take turns guessing who or what the other groups are. Animals of any kind are fun, but so are modes of transportation, musical instruments, different languages, cartoon characters, things in outer-space or any category from your imagination.

Charades

there are many
ways to
play charades.

There are many ways to play charades.

 Classic Charades: Children take turns drawing titles of books, movies or famous quotations out of a hat and acting them out for the group.

Picture Charades: Children take turns drawing picture flash cards out of a hat and then acting them out for the group. (This version is much easier for children who speak different languages or read at different levels.)

Lemonade: Children get into partners or small groups and decide on an occupation or activity to act out ("Let's be building a house" or "We can be sailors"). When they are ready they walk toward each other chanting: "Lemonade What's Your Trade?" several times. Then they take turns performing for each other and guessing each other's actions. They then can find new partners and play over again.

Same Old Story: Children divide into two groups and each group picks a well known movie or story to act out. The other group guesses while they act out the story.

Fingerspelling, Bliss Symbols, Semaphore, Morse Code And Braille

Learning new codes and then giving each other messages is a lot of fun. This is also a great chance for children who use augmentative and alternative communication systems to move into a leadership role by helping the other children become fluent in their communication systems. Also see **Secret Code Relay** (page 106).

UNDERSTANDING IN ANY LANGUAGE

Language Learning

An important way to build bridges across differences is to learn each other's languages. Exchanging languages often leads to the creation of new "pidgin" languages that combine words and grammar from each different language. For example, Deaf and Hearing children often build bridges by communicating in a combination of signing, gestures, spoken words, body language and facial expression. It's not fluent Sign Language or fluent spoken language, but it is something new that they have learned from each other. Students in exchange programs and other bilingual settings often follow a similar bridge-building strategy. Inclusive groups are open to this flexible exchange of languages rather than worrying too much about flawless grammar and vocabulary. Here are some games and activities that provide opportunities to learn each other's languages.

Exchanging languages often leads to the creation of new "pidgin" languages that combine words and grammar from each different language.

- **Language To Music:** Teach each other songs in different languages.

- **Language Clues:** Go on scavenger hunts where the clues are written in both languages or are given in pictures.

- **Card Games:** Speak both languages while playing cards and board games.

- **Food For Thought:** Learn each other's language while cooking and sharing food together

- **Pictures Of Our Lives:** Look through photo albums and magazines. Learn words and phrases from each other's languages while looking at pictures.

- **Show Me A Story:** Act out simple stories twice; first in one language, then in the other.

- **Interpreter Support:** Get together with the help of an interpreter to have a fluent conversation.

- **Hidden Object:** Send one or two children out of the room while the rest of the children hide an object. When they return give clues, first in one language then in another, until they find the object.

- **Crafty Communication:** Take turns demonstrating crafts or customs while speaking the languages used at home. Encourage the other children to copy what is said as well as what is demonstrated.

- **Potato People:** Get potatoes, carrots, celery and other vegetables. Gather pipe cleaners, thumb-tacks and other craft supplies. Exchange vocabulary while making characters together.

- **Friendship Collage:** Bring in magazines written in several different languages. Make friendship collages by cutting out pictures and words from these magazines.

- **Multilingual Pictionary:** Translate the words in a pictionary game into several different languages.

Secret Sounds

Explore sound codes invented by children from around the world. Encourage children to crack the codes below and then speak or write the code by applying the rule to other words and sentences. Some children learn to carry on long conversations in these secret sound codes. Also see **Secret Code Relay** (page 106).

Here are the English words *"Dare to be different"* written in several different sound codes:

 "Ku-dare ku-to ku-be ku-diff-ku-er-ku-ent"
(**Ku** was invented by Russian children)

"Ip-dare ip-to ip-be ip-diff-ip-er-ip-ent"
(**Ip** was invented by Jamaican children)

"Are-day oo-tay ee-bay ifferent-day"
(**Pig Latin** was invented by American children)

"Dare to be ent-er-diff"
(**Kinyume** was invented by East African children)

"Dare-lare-sare to-loo-soo be-lee-see diff-liff-siff er-ler-ser ent-lent-sent"
(**Sa-la** was invented by Chinese children)

"Dod-a-ror-e tot-oo bob-ee dod-i-fof-fof-e-ror-e-non-tot"
(**Funny Bone** was invented by children in Germany)

Listeners try
to understand the
key ideas and
reflect back
the feelings
they are hearing.

Remember When

Help children get into small groups and exchange stories about important events in their lives. Children often enjoy remembering events while looking through photo-albums, showing souvenirs or reading stories and letters they or their relatives have written about important events. Listeners try to understand the key ideas and reflect back the feelings they are hearing.

From Our Point Of View

In this game with many variations, children practice translating from images to words and/or body language and then back again. The basic set up is to have drawings, designs, photographs, sculptures or objects that are visible to some children but hidden from the rest. The children who can see what is hidden describe what they see. The rest of the children can be challenged to respond in several ways:

- guess what is being described
- ask questions to learn more about what is being described
- select what is being described from a number of choices
- re-create what is being described by drawing or constructing it

Also see **Off-Stage Drawing** (page 105).

Walk And Talk

Provide opportunities for two or three children to go for a walk together and talk about life, the universe and everything. Instead of pointing to and naming objects, ask them to focus on learning about interests, dislikes, relationships and activities.

Doctor Dolittle

Doctor Dolittle could communicate with every animal on earth. Children can too. It is all a matter of taking their time and opening up all their senses.

Gather a group of children together and instruct them to go for a long walk or sit quietly in one place for awhile. Encourage everyone to, "Pay attention, relax and use all your senses as you learn to understand the many, many languages of the natural world. What can you each learn about the language of a river, the wind, the trees or a caterpillar? How many different bird calls can you identify? How do plants and animals communicate through their actions and through more subtle languages such as changes in color? How do different plants, animals and natural forces communicate with each other?" After children have spent some time listening to nature's many languages, get together and share what you have learned.

Listen To The Earth

Visit scientists and amateur naturalists in your community and get them to show you the different instruments they use to watch and listen to nature. Some instruments are thermometers, barometers, stethescopes, magnifying glasses, telescopes, microscopes, radios, metal detectors, seismographs and cameras. Encourage children to try out some of these instruments on their own or with supervision. Taking the time to watch and listen to nature is incredibly surprising and builds immense respect.

Pay attention, relax and use all your senses as you learn to understand the many, many languages of the natural world.

Learn each other's languages while cooking and sharing food together.

TUNING IN

During a science lesson about astronomy Pam, who has low vision, told us about the time she saw a star. She described how Melanie, her camp counsellor took her outside one dark and moonless night to a huge field, far away from the city lights. They turned off their flashlights and Melanie helped Pam point binoculars up into the heavens. *"The star that I found was bright and beautiful and it shone right into my eye."* By tuning in to Melanie, Pam was able to discover something she had never ever seen before. As we listened with empathy, we were all able to experience the miraculous joy she felt when she looked up through those binoculars and saw a star for the very first time.

by Lisa Kruk, age 11

FROM **LINK MAGAZINE** (1991) HONIARA: SOLOMON ISLANDS DEVELOPMENT TRUST. REPRINTED WITH PERMISSION.

THE BOYS FROM BANAFOU BAY

DIS TAEM MOSKITO PLANTI TU MAS, IUMI MAS KILIM OLKETA..

TUFALA IA TOK TOK NATING, HEMI HAD FO KILIM MOSKITO SAPOS TUFALA NO KLINIM RAONIM VILIJ!!...

THERE ARE TOO MANY MOSQUITOES IN OUR VILLAGE. WHAT A PAIN!

BOY, IT'S HARD TO FIND ENOUGH MOSQUITOES TO EAT IN A CLEAN VILLAGE. WHAT A PAIN!

Tyler Shaw was only eleven years old when he and his family found out he had acquired AIDS from a blood transfusion. On top of dealing with their grief about his illness, the Shaw family had to deal with prejudice against AIDS. Tyler and his older siblings were rejected by almost all their formerly friendly schoolmates. At first their household — which had always been the neighborhood gathering spot — felt overwhelmingly sad, empty and lost. The phone stopped ringing and the kids were targets of name calling, hate mail, threats, and physical assaults. But Mr. and Mrs. Shaw kept their doors open as always and, within a few weeks, young people began to gather again. There were many new faces. The Shaw kitchen became a drop-in center for boys who were harrassed for being too effeminate, teens whose different sexual orientation meant rejection from their own families, and children who were teased because their parents, aunts or uncles were Gay or Lesbian. For the Shaw family, the difficult process of tuning into their child's struggles with his illness, was also a process of tuning into the struggles faced by all children who deal with homophobia.

SKILL 11: TUNING IN

Just like tuning up musical instruments together, tuning in prepares people to join in harmony with each other. Tuning in means:

- becoming fully absorbed in what the other person is communicating with their heart, mind, actions and words

- putting ourselves in the other person's place to experience the strengths as well as the challenges of their journey

- communicating empathy with our hearts, minds, actions and words

Inclusive leaders acknowledge, accept and value the input of everyone in a group so that everyone has opportunities to:

- open up to each other

- listen to each other with respect

- interact as equals

- understand each person's different point of view

- adjust activities to accommodate everyone's input

When children are in tune, they can all be heard. Now understanding can deepen and beautiful possibilities can begin to emerge.

When children are in tune, they can all be heard.

Tip: Inclusive leaders know that showing compassion and empathy do not necessarily mean agreement and following along. Tuning into another person's situation while continuing to play a different tune or follow a different rhythm is complex but very possible.

Here are several cooperative games, creative activities and adventures in nature that give children enjoyable opportunities to tune in to their interconnections with each other.

Radar

This game is a fast moving way of developing the concentration needed to tune in to sounds. At the same time children learn about the skill of echo location used by bats, owls, killer whales, dolphins and other animals to find their food. Have the children get into a circle and select one child to be blindfolded. This child is now a predator who uses echoes to find food. Select a few children to be a kind of prey the predator likes to eat. The rest of the children establish the boundaries of the eco-system by standing in a large circle around the animals.

Whenever the predator calls out "Radar," the prey all call back "Beep" in high pitched radar-like voices. The predator uses the feedback from the beeps to search out and tag the prey. (The prey join the boundary circle when they are tagged.) In the meantime, the circle of children make the game easier or harder by adjusting the size of their boundaries.

Once everyone can play this game safely with one predator, children may want to try playing with two predators and a few more prey. This version requires the predators to cooperate and the circle of children to be alert spotters to help prevent collisions.

Children learn to tune in to movement, touch and non-verbal social cues.

Thumbs-Up

In **Thumbs-Up**, children learn to tune in to movement, touch and non-verbal social cues. Three or more children stand in front of the group and call out "Heads down, thumbs up." (In a large group, when seven children are chosen at a time, this game is known as **Seven-Up**.)

The rest of the children close their eyes, put their heads down and their thumbs up and wait while the thumb-touchers walk through the group and each touch one child's thumb. When a child's thumb is touched he or she raises it in the air.

When all the thumb-touchers have touched someone's thumb, they return to the front of the group and call out: "Thumbs down, Heads up."

Now the children whose thumbs were touched guess who touched them. If the guess is correct, they trade places.

Tell By Touch

This old-time game, commonly known as **Blindman's Buff** (or **Bluff**), gives children practice tuning in to physical features. One child volunteers to be blindfolded and is spun around in the center of the circle a few times. To add to the disorientation, the other children quickly exchange places and shift the circle around. Now the blindfolded person puts hands out in front and walks slowly from the center to the edge of the group. Eventually he touches someone and guesses who it is by feeling that person's face, hair and clothing.

Where Is The Ring Bearer?

Children from many different countries enjoy tuning into subtle movements and body language while playing this traditional game that involves strategy as well as guessing. A small ring is suspended on a wide circle of string that everyone holds with both hands. One child goes into the middle of the circle and tries to follow the whereabouts of the ring as it gets passed along the string from hand to hand around the circle. This is easier said than done because players:

- try to conceal the ring when it comes to them

- pretend that they have the ring when they don't

- change the direction and speed of the ring as it is passed

- lift and lower the string

Some children enjoy playing **Where Is The Ring Bearer?** while singing songs and giving the child in the middle a turn to guess at the end of each verse.

If the child makes a guess that turns out to be wrong, then the non-ring-bearer comes into the middle to help out. Once found, the ring bearer comes into the middle, everyone who was in the middle goes back to the circle to hold onto the string and the ring begins to travel from ring bearer to ring bearer again.

sharing music, movement and rhythms together can really get a diverse group in tune with each other.

Notice The Difference?

This game challenges children to tune in their powers of observation. Children get into two groups and line up facing each other. One group turns around and hides their eyes while the other team changes something subtle about their appearance (e.g. sleeves rolled up, arms folded a different way, collars up instead of down, noses wrinkled, one eye closed, hats exchanged). Once the first team guesses what is different, it is their turn to make a change.

Rhythm And Movement Jam Sessions

Sharing music, movement and rhythms together can really get a diverse group in tune with each other and with specific group members. The basic idea is that one person starts making a sound or movement (such as doing a dance step, humming a tune, strumming a cord, drumming a beat or making an action). Others join in as they feel ready. Together the group strives to absorb, tune in to and add on to each other's sounds and movements. Here are a few of many variations.

- Children take turns conducting the group.

- Children jam with musical instruments, rhythm instruments or homemade instruments from the kitchen, workshop or garden shed.

- Two or three groups play music back and forth to each other.

- One group provides the music while the other group responds with movement, dance, drama or drawing.

- The sessions get videotaped or tape-recorded.

Unfinished Pictures

This two-part art activity gives children opportunities to tune in to different points of view. First children make several ambiguous or unfinished pictures. They could make pictures in many different ways.

- Make ink blots by putting a glob of finger paint in the middle of a sheet of paper and folding it over.

- Draw a few lines and shapes on a page.

- Cover up most of a page out of a coloring book with white paint or white paper, leaving only some of the lines showing.

To prepare for the second part of the activity, number the pages, photocopy them, collate them into sets and distribute them to individual children or to children who will be working together in pairs or small groups. Each child or small group of children gets a complete set of all the pages.

Now the pictures are ready to be finished. Individually or in pairs, everyone works on the same ambiguous drawing at the same time, without looking over at what the other children are doing. Once everyone has completed a picture they compare their outcomes, noticing where they all had the same interpretation and where their viewpoints were quite different.

There are many card games that help children develop their abilities to understand and express emotions.

Emotional Flash Cards

There are many card games that help children develop their abilities to understand and express emotions. First make a stack of about fifty flash cards that each have the word for an emotion and a picture that illustrates that emotion. Here are some examples of emotions.

- *Happy Emotions:* excited, satisfied, comfortable, confident.

- *Sad Emotions:* upset, disappointed, missing someone, wistful.

- *Scared Emotions:* embarrassed, afraid, nervous, confused.

- *Angry Emotions:* bugged, grumpy, fed up, hot and bothered.

Get children involved in adding to these lists of words that describe emotions and in making the flashcards. Children can make two or more cards for the same emotion if they want. They can illustrate the words by cutting pictures out of magazines, drawing pictures of faces showing different feelings, making up symbols and colors that go with different emotions or making cartoons that show characters acting out different emotions.

Now they are ready to play cards. Here are a few games that can all be played individually or in partners:

- **Feelings Charades**: This game helps children explore how to communicate feelings through body language and facial expression. Children take turns picking a card and then non-verbally acting out that feeling for the other players to guess.

🦋 **Feelings Fish:** Deal some cards to each person. The rest go in the middle. Children take turns fishing for a pair as in this example: Mathieu says, "Tanya, do you have a card that goes with my shy card?" Tanya looks through her cards. She can either give Mathieu a card that goes with "shy" in some way (any match is just fine so long as the children can think of a connection) or she could say "Go Fish." Once Mathieu has received a card or fished for a card in the center pile, he sets any matching pairs aside and the turn passes to the child on the left. Play until someone runs out of cards then count up all the pairs for a collective score.

🦋 **Feelings Concentration:** Children lay out all of the cards face down on the table. The first child turns over two cards and tries to figure out a way that the two feelings are connected. If yes, then he or she keeps the pair of cards. If not, the cards get turned face down again. Either way, the turn passes on to the next child. If they want, children can count their pairs once all the cards have been picked up.

Passing on a turn is just fine and going around the circle two or three times is just fine too.

Talking Circle

In a talking circle, each person, in order, has a turn to hold a "talking" stick or other object and share how they feel and what they are thinking about. Everyone else tunes in by listening with their eyes, ears, hearts and minds and by trying to put themselves in the same place as the person who is talking. There is no pressure to share, passing on a turn is just fine and going around the circle two or three times is just fine too.

Sharing Traditions

Peace and harmony build when people trust each other enough to tune in to each other's important traditions (but see **Caution** sidebar for advice on obtaining permission first). Traditions can be shared through:

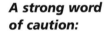 **A strong word of caution:** *Many important traditions are sacred and cultural appropriation (taking over aspects of another culture without permission) is a big problem that can be very hurtful. For these reasons, it is essential to ask for guidance from parents and elders when sharing traditions and ceremonies.*

🦋 stories, photographs, videos and demonstrations

🦋 visiting each other's homes, churches and community centers

🦋 attending special open events such as when a cultural center invites members of the wider community to come and share

Magnifying Nature's Beauty

Borrow magnifying glasses and take children out into the field to tune in to the small things in life. Encourage everyone to kneel on the ground, shrink their perspectives down to the size of a bumble bee and let their senses and imaginations fly along close to the ground for an aerial view of the world of bugs, grass and moss.

BRINGING IN THE REINFORCEMENTS

I asked a group of students to explain how they learned and remembered things. They told me that they learn what they love.

"I can easily learn and remember anything if I am interested in it. I love playing sports. I go over and over each step many times. I practice until I know I'm better." (Raymond)

"First I watch, then I practice for a couple of hours and if I really enjoy it, I learn it. Like, when I first tried a bicycle I didn't know how to balance, but after a few days of practicing, I learned how to balance and ride." (Dominic)

"If I play a game, I easily learn very fast, but if I stay back and watch, I won't know it. Then, once I know the actions and the rules of a game, I can remember best if I show other people how to play." (Joseph)

"I like weaving when someone does it with me. I follow along as I watch and listen. It's easiest for me when I'm weaving with people because it makes it more fun to just continue on practicing along with everyone else." (Lorena)

"To learn poems I write. My mom knows I'm a writer so she lets me write the words on paper, in books, or anywhere I want to — even the walls if I wash it off later." (Marcia)

"I learn songs easily because I sing almost all the time. When I'm alone, I just sing and sing while I'm doing things. When I'm with other kids, we all sing together." (Rupinder)

Crystal used to be known by the other students as "the girl who reads at lunch hour" because she tried to deal with her loneliness by sitting on the school steps and reading books. When James tried to deal with his loneliness by chasing after her, she gave up being a book worm and refused to go to school at all. This is when her mom and teachers asked me to bring in the reinforcements. I helped her make a list of classmates she would like to get along with. Her list included several girls she wanted to play with and several boys — including James — she wanted to stop being so rough. We then invited these students to form a "Building Friendly Bridges Club" and they all signed up. At the end of only six lunch hours of learning through play, Crystal was bubbling about how things had turned around on the playground. *"Building bridges is lots and lots of fun! I'm not playing by myself anymore, because people are letting people play with them now. Like, if somebody doesn't have someone to play with them, they just ask somebody! Building friendly bridges helps all of us to play along."* James also learned a lot over six weeks, but gave the credit to everyone else. *"I think building bridges is good because people are more civilized, not like a bunch of monkeys. Some kids have been acting a lot better than they usually do. I noticed a couple of kids can maybe play better and maybe play with me sometimes. If you go through these social skills often enough they can be put into practice and used. I think that everybody knows them — some more than others — it's putting them into action that a lot of people need to work on."*

SKILL 12: BRINGING IN THE REINFORCEMENTS

BRINGING IN THE REINFORCEMENTS

One of my favorite cooperative activities is for us to collectively build a bridge from one place to another. As we figure out how to reinforce the connections that prevent everything from collapsing we are learning about the effects of supportive reinforcement over and over again.

Whether or not actions are strengthened or weakened depends on the immediate consequences. Actions that lead to positive results get strengthened. People will continue to do things that result in these kinds of effects.

- *Pleasant Physical Sensations:* a good taste, a nice smell, a beautiful sight, a pleasant touch.

- *Enjoyable Emotional Feelings:* relaxation, excitement, an adrenaline rush, relief, satisfaction.

- *Mastery or Success:* finishing a task, getting something to work, figuring something out, getting something to balance, doing something that seems 'just right'.

- *Positive Social Feedback:* praise, pats on the back, smiles, thanks, cheers, jokes, laughter.

Actions that lead to positive results get strengthened.

There are two keys to helping children develop strength and confidence through positive feedback.

- Provide plenty of opportunity for children to do things that lead to positive results.

- Surround them with parents, relatives, teachers, friends and other people who know how to bring in the reinforcements over and over and over again.

Tip: Bringing in the reinforcements is a very effective way of preventing risks from becoming realities. Involving children in adventurous, fun and successful activities builds strong self esteem, confidence and resilience.

Here are some enjoyable indoor and outdoor activities that show the reinforcing power of immediate feedback.

Begin with small groups of four or five children and increase the length of the rope and the numbers of children pulling together as cooperation builds.

Rope Shapes

In a **Rope Shapes** activity, children learn to pull together to give effective feedback by holding onto a circle of rope and then cooperating together to make different shapes. Begin with small groups of four or five children and increase the length of the rope and the numbers of children pulling together as cooperation builds.

- For a triangle, everyone pulls gently to keep the rope tight in three directions.
- For a circle everyone keeps the rope evenly spaced.
- A square needs children to pull equal sections of the rope in four different directions.
- With practice, children will figure out how to make more complex shapes such as hexagons, stars, numbers and letters.

There are many ways to make pulling together more complicated.

- Everyone can try to sit down and then stand up together while maintaining a shape.
- Children can use several ropes to make mazes and then take turns running through them.
- Children can create rope dances by making sequences of shapes in time to music.
- Instead of using rope, children can make shapes by linking hands or holding onto scarves.

Booby Trap

This variation on the pen and paper game of **Battleship** is a journey through a dangerous swamp, an underground cavern, a spooky woods or any other scary voyage you can imagine. Help children get ready by marking out a large grid on the ground with chalk or with long ropes or pieces of string. Each square in the grid should be about two feet by two feet.

Now children get into partners or small groups and draw secret maps, coloring in squares that are connected vertically, horizontally or diagonally to show a safe route from one side of the grid to the other.

Keeping their map hidden, one group challenges the rest of the children to find their safe route through the maze.

The children line up and the courageous child who is first in line steps into a square. The children with the map give immediate feedback by saying "Safe" or "Booby-Trap." "Safe" means that the explorer has been fortunate enough to step into a square that corresponds to a colored square on the map. "Booby-trap!" means the explorer has ventured off the route into unmarked territory. The feedback of "Safe" is a signal to step on another square. The signal of "Booby-trap" sends the explorer back to the end

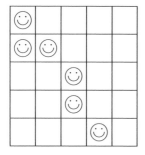

Sample map showing the safe route through a 5 by 5 grid.

of the line. Either way, the entire line up of children have learned something about the route and the safe places to step are reinforced.

Now the second child tries. This child will get a little farther before stepping into a "booby-trap." Now it is the next child's turn.

Each child will advance a little farther because of learning from the preceding children's trials and errors. Once one person gets across safely, the rest of the children will be able to follow the route across without too much difficulty.

After everyone is across, the next group of map-makers challenges everyone to try to get back over to the other side by figuring out another safe route through the maze.

BRINGING
IN THE
REINFORCEMENTS

You Are Getting Warmer!

Children learn from feedback in this simple game of hide and seek. One or two children leave the room while everyone else hides a small object. Then the seeker returns and starts searching while being guided by feedback from the hiders. "Cold" means the child is far away from the hidden object. "Warm" means getting close. "Hot" means the child is almost on top of the missing item and "boiling" means the child is practically touching the object!

A much more challenging variation on this feedback game is for two or more children to leave the room while everyone decides on a secret action for them to do (for example the secret action could be to stand on a chair). The children come back and help each other discover the secret action by trying out various actions while receiving feedback from the group (cold, warm, hot, boiling). With patience, perseverance and accurate feedback, actions that are closer and closer to the secret will be reinforced and the children will eventually figure out the secret action without being told.

With patience, perseverance and accurate feedback, actions that are closer and closer to the secret will be reinforced.

Louder And Louder

Reinforcing volume control is a good way of practicing taking turns, public speaking and remembering people's names at the same time. One person says their name, the next person repeats the name louder, the next repeats it louder and so on, right round the circle. Now, the name goes back the other way with each child saying it a little more quietly each time until it fades to a whisper.

Cooperative Cards

Strengthen self esteem and build confidence while making cooperative greeting cards in this cooperative drawing activity. Also see **Cooperative Drawing** (page 23).

To start, each child folds a piece of paper into a card shape, writes their name on the inside and draws a picture on the outside.

Next each person passes their card to the right. Children add to the picture and write positive messages about the person whose name is inside the card. Then they pass the card to the right again. The cooperative drawing and affirmative writing continues until each person has their original card back.

Finally each child reads the positive messages they have received from each member of the group. They may want to read them silently or they may want to share them aloud.

BRINGING IN THE REINFORCEMENTS

Video Feedback

Sports coaches and drama teachers know that video taping children as they learn new skills is a very effective coaching technique. Many coaches use video demonstrations and video feedback to guide children to learn complex stunts and sequences of movements. You can slow stunts down by showing videos in slow motion, you can use the pause feature to break skills into smaller steps and you can show children videos of themselves. Video feedback is especially effective if the coach takes the time to edit all the mistakes out so that children only watch and think about their successful scenes. Video children as they practice connecting skills. Edit the videos and then reinforce their connecting skills by showing them the successful highlights.

Positive Exaggeration

This positive feedback game that reinforces confidence and optimism is a variation on the well known game of **Broken Telephone** except that the message is deliberately exaggerated in a positive direction and is passed around the group aloud so that everyone can hear.

The first child shares some neutral or positive information. The second child passes this message along to the third child, exaggerating the information in a positive way. The third child exaggerates the message a little more and passes it on to the fourth child. Here is an example of how this game would be played in a group of ten children.

It is amazing how strong and confident each person feels about their potential to be great after taking a turn listening to their accomplishments being positively exaggerated.

> Child 1 taps Child 2 on the shoulder and says, *"I like playing basketball."*
>
> Child 2 taps Child 3 on the shoulder and says, *"Hey, did you hear that Sara is one cool basketball player?"*
>
> Child 3 taps Child 4 on the shoulder and says, *"Hey, did you hear that Sara is in the running for the all-star basketball team?"*
>
> Child 4 taps Child 5 on the shoulder and says, *"Hey, did you hear that Sara made 12 baskets in a row in last night's game?"*
>
> Child 5 taps Child 6 on the shoulder and says, *"Hey, did you hear that Sara was the most valuable player for an entire month?"*
>
> Child 6 taps Child 7 on the shoulder and says, *"Hey, did you read the story in the newspaper about Sara getting picked for the Olympic basketball team!"*
>
> Child 8 taps Child 9 on the shoulder and says, *"Hey, did you hear that Sara won a basketball scholarship to Australia!"*
>
> Child 9 taps Child 10 on the shoulder and says, *"Hey, I think it was Sara I saw playing basketball on television last night!"*

It is amazing how strong and confident each person feels about their potential to be great after taking a turn listening to their accomplishments being positively exaggerated.

Who Could this Be?

This guessing game really builds up children's self esteem. The first step is to collect positive feedback about each child. One way is to write children's names on envelopes and tape them on the door. Throughout the day or the week, children secretly put positive messages in the envelopes. Once there are at least a few positive messages in each child's envelope, you are ready to play the guessing game. Children gather together. Without showing whose envelope it is, someone reads out the positive messages from that envelope one by one until that child is identified and given a big round of applause. Go on to the next envelope and continue playing until each person has been identified and applauded. This game can be played again and again as more and more reinforcing clues are added. The clues can eventually be pasted onto a poster and presented to each child as a reminder of how much they are valued.

BRINGING IN THE REINFORCEMENTS

reinforcing Poetry

Children enjoy writing poetry that strengthens their passions for the things they love to do. There are many different poetic formats. Here are two simple examples.

Continue playing until each person has been identified and applauded.

Activity Poems: A child thinks of something he or she loves to do and writes that word or phrase vertically down the left hand side of a piece of paper. Each letter becomes the first letter of a sentence about that activity.

> *SWIMMING!*   BY DEANNA HILL, AGE 12
>
> *Swimming is so much fun*
> *When I swim I am very happy*
> *In swimming lessons you learn how to swim*
> *Many people take swimming lessons*
> *Many people are very talented swimmers*
> *I am one of the many who LOVE swimming*
> *Nutty people would jump off the high diving board*
> *   if they did not know how to swim*
> *Good swimmers would be able to jump off the diving board*

Name Poems: Children can make up poems about each other following this sample 7-line format (feel free to substitute other characteristics):

Name...	*CLAIRE* BY DEANNA HILL, AGE 12
Positive descriptive words...	*Funny, nice, happy, peaceful, friendly*
Relationships with others...	*Friend of Deanna, Jackie, Ally*
Loves and passions...	*Lover of cats, swimming, rain, chocolate,* *soccer balls, pets*
Gifts...	*Gives trust, laughter, respect*
Dreams...	*Dreams of dolphins, eclipses and Disneyland*
Name...	*Our friend CLAIRE!*

freeze!

Children learn to notice the natural reinforcers that sustain life in this game. Everyone spreads out singly or in partners to explore a natural area. One person stands in the middle of the area and makes a "freeze" signal such as blowing a whistle or waving a flag every few moments. When the signal to freeze is made, everyone else stops their explorations completely, stands totally still, closes their eyes and holds their breath for as long as possible. Children start breathing and exploring until the whistle blows again. After everyone has gone through this explore-freeze-explore sequence several times, everyone gathers together and compares what happened during the *explore* phase (when many actions and sensations were being reinforced to what happened during the *freeze* phase (when nothing was being reinforced).

GIVING
A HAND

On the fourth day of our Children's Group at the Cowichan Tribes TseWulTun Health Center, all the children and their teenage coaches had just finished cutting wet deer skin into long thin strips that would eventually be used to lace up their drums. Garrett and I were feeling pretty good about how well everyone had formed into a cohesive, respectful group. Everyone except for Ray, that is. Ray had not only missed the second and third days of the group, he seemed to have missed out on the entire bonding process and so he was still an outsider. So far today his main contributions had been to interrupt the opening prayer by arriving late; trip his cousin Amanda during a game of Frozen Tag; knock a chair over during the story of Tzouhalem the Frog Mountain; and chop his deer skin up into tiny pieces, saying "Look, I'm making deer droppings." Now he was barging into the front of the line of children who were politely waiting to get their snacks. As I struggled against my strong desire to tell him to smarten up or go home, I tried to figure out how to offer him a hand. *"Hey Garrett, Ray is still almost like a guest in the Children's Group. How do Cowichan people serve food to guests?"* Garrett picked up my idea and ran with it, *"We welcome our guests by sitting them in a place of honour and serving them the best food. Come and sit down Ray. I will serve you in the Cowichan way."* Garrett then seated him in the big comfortable arm chair that the Elders always sat in and personally served him his snack. As Ray realized that he was being treated as THE most important person in the whole room, he looked up at Garrett with an expression of worship. He beamed as he politely drank his juice and ate his cheese and crackers. Then he stood up and went around the circle, offering to share his big bowl of grapes with everyone. We could all see that Garrett's respectful, helping hand had been just what Ray needed to be able to jump over his nervousness and land in the group with both feet on the ground and his arms open wide.

Making drums

Meomeo – *Children*
Au tarimai haku – *Put out your net for me.*
Meomeo – *Children*
Vake rae Kori niu – *I can scrape coconut for you.*
Meomeo – *Children*
Kori niu marimari – *Scraping sweet coconut.*
Meomeo – *Children*
Ta i paruahea – *Then loose your net.*
Meomeo – *Children*

(ARE'ARE FOLK SONG, SOLOMON ISLANDS)

SKILL 13: GIVING A HAND

If you have ever heard the protest, "I can do it myself!", you know that giving a hand without taking over can be a delicate balancing act. Your helping hand will only be effective if it guides a child to safety or leads the way to more choice, more power or more fun. Remember that any gift, including a helping hand, can only be offered. Unless it is an emergency, it is up to the child to accept or reject a helping hand.

GIVING A HAND

When you offer your hands to help a child it is important to remember to:

- give a calm and relaxed hand (not a tense or impatient push)
- help the child to experience success and mastery without providing so much help that the child becomes helpless
- partner with the child so that you are each doing part of the job
- fade your help until the child can do it as independently as possible

Remember that any gifts, including a helping hand, can only be offered... it is up to the child to accept or reject a helping hand.

There are many ways of giving a hand.

- Give something to the child such as a toy, a tool, or a wheelchair.
- Do something for the child such as tying shoelaces, or making a sandwich.
- Provide hand over hand support.
- Give a light touch to cue a child about what to do next.
- Show what to do by gesturing or signalling.
- Give a comforting or supportive hug.

A strong word of caution:
Be very careful not to use your hands to restrain, restrict or force a child except when the child or others are in immediate danger.

GIVING
A HAND

Here are several games and activities that involve children in giving each other a hand.

Frozen Tag

The challenge is for the players to avoid being tagged while they are helping each other. These variations on the classic game encourage creative teamwork:

- **Dead Ant:** Show the boundaries of the play area and select one or two children to be spiders. The rest of the children are ants. The spider is trying to get all the ants in a web by running after them and tagging them. When someone is tagged, they do what helpless ants caught in a web do: They lie on their back and wave their arms in the air. They can only be saved if four fellow ants can come over and each hold on to an arm or a leg. Then, they quickly help the ant turn over and run away from the spider. The game ends when the spider(s) have tagged all the ants.

- **Hug Tag:** Children cannot be frozen if they are hugging each other and one child can unfreeze another child with a hug.

- **Bean Bag Tag:** Children walk around the room with bean bags on their heads. The chasers are allowed to pick their bean bags up if they drop them, but the rest of the children need to stop and wait for a helpful passer-by when they are tagged or when they drop their bean bag.

- **Trick or Treat:** Children can be unfrozen if someone who is not frozen applauds while they perform a trick such as a hand stand, a magic trick, a song or a dance.

- **Antidote:** Children can sprinkle an unfreezing potion on anyone who is frozen.

- **Make Up:** Children can make up their own unfreezing rule and create a brand new game of frozen tag.

Make a rule
that getting hit
above the waist
doesn't count
so that the balls
stay low.

Doctor Dodge Ball

Draw lines or lay skipping ropes to divide the play area into three sections. A few children go on each side to be the throwers, most of the children go in the middle to be the dodgers and one or two children on the side lines are the doctors (who are immune from the effects of any stray balls). The throwers try to hit the dodgers with soft rubber balls. If someone gets hit by the ball (make a rule that getting hit above the waist doesn't count so that the balls stay low), they fall down in a show of great agony. A doctor runs out and helps the person stand up and limp over to the side-lines where they quickly recover and run back in to the middle again. (Children can shift from one position to another any time.)

Navigating Bridges

When children go hiking, they practice giving each other a hand whenever they help each other navigate along a log, step from stone to stone, go along a narrow walkway, climb up a steep path or meet other natural challenges. Indoors or on a playground children can create challenging routes by using existing cracks and lines, chalk, rope, boards, benches or flat stones to lay out narrow bridges across imaginary creeks and canyons. In the summer at the beach or during any season in a pool, children can have a lot of fun creating a wobbly bridge of inner tubes or air mattresses. On a wobbly bridge, just getting across with help is enough of a challenge. On a less difficult bridge, children think up balancing challenges that require at least two people. Here are a few examples.

GIVING
A HAND

- Each person holds onto one end of a pole while balancing a hat in the middle.

- Each person holds a ball between two hockey sticks.

- Each person holds a piece of newspaper tight while balancing a water balloon in the middle.

- Children can get into two groups on opposite sides of the bridge. Beginning at the same time, the challenge is for everyone to keep each other safely on the narrow path while crossing from one side to the other. If someone slips off and touches the ground, everyone goes back to the beginning and tries again — more carefully this time.

the challenge is for everyone to keep each other safely on the narrow path while crossing from one side to the other.

Secret Agent

Call out each child's name and say "I have a secret mission for you". Whisper something the child can do to be helpful for the next few minutes. Below are some examples of secret missions.

- "Make a birthday card for Tasha."
- "Sweep the floor for Misty."
- "Put the chairs away."
- "Take the dog for a walk."
- "Offer each person a cookie."
- "Display the art work on the wall."

Help Wanted

Set up a bulletin board or advertising flyer and encourage children to submit *Help Wanted* and *Want to Help Ads*. *Help Wanted Ads* ask for help.

- "If you can teach me to play the ukulele please contact Gus."
- "If you can help me practice basketball meet me at the basketball court any recess. Yours truly, Sylvie."
- "I want to visit William in hospital but I need a ride. If your parents can drive me please phone Brent at 555-6141."

Want to Help Ads offer help.

- "I want to read to younger kids. If you like listening to stories and you live close to Market Street I can come to your house. My name is Leslie. My phone number is 555-3321."

(continued on the next page)

GIVING
A HAND

Posting short articles or making announcements about successful helping arrangements will encourage these mutually supportive relationships.

(Help Wanted continued)

🖐 "I can teach cool piano duets to anyone. We can use the piano in the school music room before school and at lunch hour. If you want to learn you can find me in Division 207. Michiko."

🖐 "I love animals. If you need someone to look after your pets, call me at 555-5587 and ask for Rita."

Posting short articles or making announcements about successful helping arrangements will encourage these mutually supportive relationships.

Shoe Twister

In this game, each child removes one shoe and puts it in a pile in the center of the room. Then everyone helps each other get the shoe back on. Some challenges that could be added are:

🖐 put shoes on while holding hands

🖐 keep your eyes closed while helping each other put shoes on

🖐 stay standing on one foot while helping each other

🖐 keep hands behind backs

Construction Zone

Construction toys and building supplies provide many opportunities to give each other a hand and build a group of solidly connected children at the same time. Here are some building projects.

🖐 Combine several construction sets to create a village with vehicles, buildings, roads and bridges.

🖐 Beginning from the four corners of the room, build bridges until they all connect up with each other.

🖐 Using a pile of newspapers and masking tape, build a shelter that is big enough for everyone to fit inside.

🖐 Build a tent city out of sheets, clothespins and rope.

🖐 Take shovels and buckets to a sandy beach and give each other a hand building a walled city complete with tunnels, moats and turrets.

Two On a Crayon

Two or more children draw a picture together in this activity for exploring interdependence and mutual help. The main rule is that both children hold on to the crayon, pencil or paintbrush at the same time. As they draw they can experiment by:

🖐 drawing with eyes closed

🖐 drawing without talking

🖐 drawing with non-dominant hands

🖐 taking turns following and leading

🕊 relaxing and waiting for the crayon to decide what to draw

🕊 inventing a holding device that will allow three, four, five or six children to hold on to the same crayon

GIVING A HAND

two or more children draw a picture together in this activity for exploring interdependence and mutual help.

Beach Clean Up

Children can give nature a hand by picking up litter at the beach or along a favorite trail. (During our local beach clean up on International Low Tide Day in May, 2000, forty-eight children and adults picked up more than three tons of litter. This works out to over one hundred pounds of all kinds of litter per person! One group even found a kitchen sink.)

Find Something Helpful

Send children out to search for about ten to twenty examples of ways living things help each other. Instead of bringing natural objects back, it is more ecologically sensitive to just bring back a list of what was observed and the location of where the observation took place. Here is a list to use as a starting point:

- *Find what birds need to be able to fly.*
- *Look for food that squirrels store to help them survive through the winter.*
- *What do baby birds need to stay safe from predators?*
- *Find something that provides a nurturing environment for baby trees to grow.*
- *What do bees need to make honey?*
- *Find things that plants need to be able to spread out their seeds.*
- *Find what baby fish need to be able to grow.*
- *What do clams need to protect themselves?*
- *Find things spiders need to survive.*

OFF-STAGE
PROMPTING

Dan withdrew into himself and became an expert at blocking people out of his awareness during many months in hospital after the car accident. The chip on his shoulder eventually grew so big that he could become invisible and invincible by ducking down behind it. From time to time he would look up long enough to steer his wheel chair into the ankles of one of the athletes who were able to play basketball while he sat on the sidelines. Things changed after a new teaching assistant came along to give him some advice behind the scenes. *"Leonard, my new TA was a really good guy. We talked a lot and he explained a lot. Because of my disabilities and the time I had spent in hospital, I had some social gaps, so he would point these things out and help me understand what was going on between people."* Leonard's advice helped Dan begin re-learning how to get along with others to the point where he eventually developed the confidence to get some of the able-bodied athletes in the community involved in wheelchair rugby.

A group of adults brainstormed about off-stage prompts we remembered hearing over and over again as children:

- Stop, look, and listen.
- Leave only footprints and take only photographs.
- Be a lover not a fighter.
- Yes, you can say No.
- If you can't say anything nice don't say anything at all.
- Smiles make the world go round.
- Put your head in gear before your mouth is in motion.
- What goes around comes around.
- Remember to flush.
- Offer to help do the dishes.
- Do not slurp spaghetti!
- It's only a game.

GROUP GROUND RULES

1. We keep each other safe by _____.
2. We make sure everyone is equal by _____.
3. We give each other choice by _____.
4. We keep this group fun by _____.

CHORE MATH

Virginia clear the table _____
Gordon stack the plates and cups _____
Cassie wipe the table _____
Evak put out cat food and water _____

Total of 4 checks = ICE CREAM CONES
for dessert!

SKILL 14: OFF-STAGE PROMPTING

OFF-STAGE PROMPTING

If life is a stage, then the important people who live, work and play with kids spend a lot of time giving off-stage directions to eager actors asking again and again: "What's next?" "What'll we do now?" Everyday life is filled with routines with unwritten scripts for children to memorize and improvise. Think of a few daily interactions such as:

- getting up and ready in the morning
- going on the bus
- going to the store
- cooking a meal

Off-stage prompting is often used to cue these routine interactions. For example, people often prompt children to say "Thank you" with the cue "What do you say now?" Signs, pictures, grocery lists and story books are other examples of off-stage prompts.

Like giving a hand, the art of giving off-stage directions is a delicate balancing act. Remember that the primary reason we communicate with each other is to exchange stories, jokes, opinions and feelings.

- Give children time to talk themselves through an activity, answer for themselves and improvise for themselves as they learn how to interact with each other.

- Fade prompts so that children can perform complex routines and participate in interactions as independently as possible.

- Give any corrective feedback in private rather than calling out a reprimand in front of the group.

Fade prompts so that children can perform complex routines and participate in interactions as independently as possible.

 Caution: *Off-stage directions should be only a very small part (less than 5%) of your interactions with any child because instructions can be interpreted as nagging or criticism.*

OFF-STAGE
PROMPTING

Here are several cooperative games and creative activities that involve children in giving and receiving off-stage prompts.

Giant Steps

Here is a game filled with off-stage prompts. Half the group lines up on one side of the room and the other half of the group lines up on the other side. Each side thinks up a name for their group (for example, "The Giants" and "The Striders"). One group calls out to the other side: "Giants, giants, what do we do next." One of the Giants calls out names and directions such as: "Gerhardt and Gina, you may take three forward baby steps and one giant sideways step." or "Everyone take ten backward hops" The Striders follow the directions and then again call out "Giants, Giants, what do we do next?" One of the giants gives more off-stage directions about who should take how many steps of what kind. The Striders gradually make their way forward, asking "What should we do next?" until one of the Giants yells "RUN BACK HOME!" The Giants then chase the Striders back home and anyone who gets tagged becomes a giant. Everyone lines up on opposite sides again and now the Giants ask "Striders, Striders, What do we do next?" and the game continues.

Life-size Tic Tac Toe

Two children are players and the rest are either naughts or crosses in this life-size version of a favorite children's board game. Children draw a large tic tac toe court on the pavement or in the sand and direct the human Xs and Os to stand where prompted.

Square Dancing

Square Dancing, Round Dancing and Contra Dancing all involve doing dance steps in response to spoken cues from a caller (as well as musical cues from accordion, banjo and fiddle music). Visit a square dancing or folk dancing club or find a dance caller in your community to come and prompt the children through a few dances.

Add-on Story Telling

In the simplest add-on story game, one person starts a story and the rest of the group members take turns adding on to it. There are many twists and turns to how children could add to each other's stories.

- **Magical Stories:** Tell a story while playing the **Magic Wand** game (page 22).

- **Believe It or Not:** Make a rule that at the end of their turn each child must say as dramatically as possible, "You'll never believe what happened next."

- **Fortunately/Unfortunately:** Someone starts by creating an unfortunate problem such as, "Unfortunately, Rita didn't feel very well when she woke up one morning." The next person solves the problem, "Fortunately, her father heard her sobs and moans." Then the next person creates another problem, "Unfortunately, he thought she was faking it." Then the next person solves the problem, "Fortunately, her pet dog realized how sick she was." And so on…

Square Dancing, Round Dancing and Contra Dancing all involve doing dance steps in response to spoken cues from a caller.

♟ **Dramatic Effect:** Create hilarious add-on stories by playing **Believe It or Not** or **Fortunately/Unfortunately** while each child pulls props out of a bag.

♟ **Tear Jerker:** Take turns picking **Emotional Flash Cards** (page 88) and make up a very emotional story.

♟ **Story Charades:** Get into two groups. One group of children tells an add-on story, while the others act it out. Also see **Charades** (page 80).

Also see **My Turn, Your Turn Story Telling** (page 58) for more story ideas.

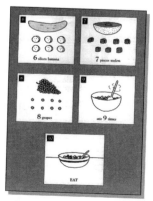
OFF-STAGE PROMPTING

Making Predictions

Children enjoy using cards to make predictions. Spades might mean work. Hearts might mean love. Diamonds might mean money. Clubs might mean nature. Each child can develop his or her own personal style of directing.

♟ "Pick a card, any card."

♟ "Count the same number of cards as your age."

♟ "Turn the cards over until you find your favorite number."

Once a few cards have been selected, children use their imaginations to link the cards together into a story about what could happen next. A queen of hearts and a seven of spades and an ace of clubs might mean something like "You will fall in love, but not until you have spent seven years working in your garden."

Each child can develop his or her own personal style of directing.

Off-Stage Drawing

In partners or small groups, one or two children draw while one or two other children tell them what to draw. Also see **From Our Point Of View** (page 82) and **Back To Front** (page 76). Try:

♟ drawing blindfolded

♟ drawing while looking in a mirror

♟ passing paper and art supplies back and forth, while taking turns directing and drawing

♟ directing other art projects such as paintings, sculptures or crafts

♟ directing others to make an exact copy of a hidden drawing or sculpture

Following Recipes

Many chefs say that learning to cook is like acting in a play with a recipe for your script. Children can get involved in cooking from a very early age and can share in all the jobs such as reading recipes, planning, shopping, measuring, chopping, mixing, shaking, decorating, tasting, cleaning up the kitchen and eating the culinary treat.

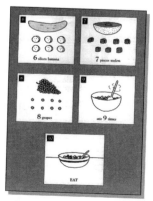

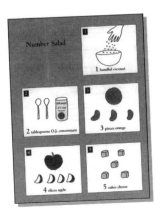

An example of a recipe that's easy to follow.

OFF-STAGE PROMPTING

Clues and riddles are fascinating off-stage prompts.

Treasure Hunts

Clues and riddles are fascinating off-stage prompts. Help children get into partners or small groups. Send each group off to hide a treasure and then work backwards toward the home-base to leave a trail of clues for others to follow. Here is how to lay out a treasure route by going to the last place first.

10. Hide the treasure.

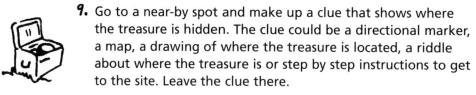

9. Go to a near-by spot and make up a clue that shows where the treasure is hidden. The clue could be a directional marker, a map, a drawing of where the treasure is located, a riddle about where the treasure is or step by step instructions to get to the site. Leave the clue there.

8. Go to another spot, a little closer to home-base and make up a clue that directs children to go to location 9.

7. Go to another spot and make up a clue that directs children to location 8.

6, 5, 4, 3, 2. Each spot is a little closer to home-base and each clue directs the finder to the next location.

1. Back at home base the children make up a clue that directs the other children to location 2.

Once each group has returned from marking out their treasure hunts, children can spend the rest of the afternoon following each pirate trail.

Secret Code Relay

In partners or small groups, children use words, codes (page 81), secret sounds (page 82), Braille or Rebus (page 78) to compose secret messages of about five to ten words long. These messages could be almost anything such as:

- a joke
- a quotation or well-known saying
- the name of a book or movie
- any other sentence

Now the children line up to receive a message from the first pair of composers. They pass the message from child to child along the line one symbol at a time. Children discuss the meaning of symbols as they pass them along. The last child tapes the symbol up on a flip chart or black-board. The challenge is to try to decipher the full message before the final off-stage prompt is passed down the line.

Social Stories

Social stories are scripts that can help children prepare for and manage challenging situations. Children enjoy role playing upcoming events such as:

- going to the dentist or the hospital
- making a speech or going to an interview
- meeting someone new or welcoming a new person into a group

- taking the bus or a plane, going on a field trip or going camping
- using a pay telephone, ordering food or buying groceries

Children will need much less off-stage prompting in real life when they have already rehearsed behind the scenes because they now know what to expect.

Blindfolded Journeys

Trust can build when one person is blindfolded and one or two responsible partners provide off-stage prompts and give a hand. Children may want to try:

- exploring while sitting on the ground until they feel confident enough to go for a walk
- walking along an established trail
- exploring off the beaten path

Individuals who live with blindness or low vision have learned a great deal about mobility orientation, sensory awareness and how to provide sensitive off-stage prompting.

I have learned the most from participating in **Blindfolded Journeys** or **Trust Walks** where one or more of the guides are blind themselves. Individuals who live with blindness or low vision have learned a great deal about mobility orientation, sensory awareness and how to provide sensitive off-stage prompting.

LEAVING OUT LOSING

Helen's counsellor found her crying within the accepting branches of the trees surrounding the outdoor chapel. *"They call me a big fat loser. Some of them tell me I should put a muzzle on my mouth so I'll stop eating, and some of them stand in a circle around me and yell 'Fat Duck, Fat Duck, Let's see you waddle.' I can't take it any more."* Stepping in to support Helen was as difficult as cleaning up the poison spread by any kind of hatred. Parents were phoned and the Camp Director and Camp Nurse sat in on a meeting between Helen and the ring leaders of the harassment. First they showed a National Film Board of Canada documentary about racism called *For Angela* (see **No-Go-Tell Videos** on page 129). The children learned that their teasing had the same impact on Helen as racial teasing had on Angela. The second step was to have the children sign contracts in which they agreed to stop teasing and to help organize a circle of support around Helen. The third step of organizing the circle of support began immediately after the meeting. Counsellors helped campers build bridges of understanding about differences by playing cooperative games in which everyone was equally included and differences were celebrated. Helen's refusal to put up with being labelled a loser helped turn her camp into a place where everyone played with each other instead of against each other.

Let every good person here join in the song.
Success to each other and pass it along.
A friend to your left and a friend to your right.
In love and good fellowship let us unite.
Now wider and wider our circle expands
We sing to our comrades in far away lands:
Vive la, vive la, vive l'amour. Vive la, vive la, vive l'amour.
Vive l'amour, vive l'amour. Vive la compagnie!

(TRADITIONAL NORTH AMERICAN SONG)

SKILL 15: LEAVING OUT LOSING

LEAVING OUT LOSING

Competition that is fun in groups of equally matched children leads to problems in diverse groups. When many different children compete against each other there will be a few children who win almost all the time, many children who lose most of the time and several children who lose almost all of the time. The children who lose out over and over again usually feel sad, scared or angry. The other children are likely to be happy about winning while feeling sad, scared or angry about (or at) the children who are losing. As the sad, scared and angry feelings build, activities that are meant to be fun become serious. Children may turn against each other, reject each other, act out or drop out.

Because of these problems associated with the effects of competition on diverse groups, it is most important for inclusive travel guides to show children how to play with each other instead of against each other. Instead of focusing on winning, losing and eliminating, children focus on:

It is most important for inclusive travel guides to show children how to play with each other instead of against each other.

- encouraging and helping each other

- giving each other lots of chances

- adapting the rules of competitive games in ways that the games are more fair for everyone

Tip: Inclusive leaders adapt games in ways that leave out losing while keeping in the excitement and enjoyment.

Here are several cooperative games, creative activities and nature experiences that leave out losing.

Cross-Over Simon Says

In traditional **Simon Says**, children who copy when the leader makes an action without saying "Simon Says" are eliminated. In **Cross-Over Simon Says**, there are two games going at once. Children who are eliminated in one game cross over and join in the other game. The children who LOVE tricking each other still get to play and the rest of the kids have way more fun running wildly back and forth from one game to the other than they ever did trying to discriminate whether or not Simon told them to do it!

Cooperative Team Sports

Any team sport such as floor hockey, basketball, volleyball, soccer or ultimate frisbee can be adapted in ways that leave out losing and keep in the fun. Here are some ways of adapting team sports in cooperative directions.

Any team sport such as floor hockey, basketball, volleyball, soccer or ultimate frisbee can be adapted in ways that leave out losing and keep in the fun.

- Match children up in opposites (more skilled players with less skilled players) and play games in partners.
- Rotate everyone through all positions so that each child takes a turn defending, scoring, being the captain, coaching, refereeing and watching.
- In games with goals, require everyone on the team to touch the ball before a goal can be counted.
- Designate a 'safe' area where players can go to rest without being penalized.
- Allow players to come back into the game after going to the end of a short line, counting to 20, saying the alphabet or singing a song.
- Omit rules or other processes that encourage hitting, shoving, pushing or other violence.
- Use different equipment such as lighter, softer or bigger balls, a lower, closer or bigger net or goal, a smaller playing area.
- Make a rule that children can put their hands up and call "Time out to invent!" at any point a game begins to feel unfair. This is a signal for children to put their heads together and adapt the rules to make the game more fun for everyone.

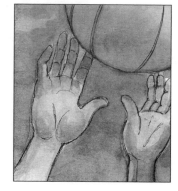

TIME OUT TO INVENT!

Cooperative Volleyball

Here are some examples of how volleyball can be adapted so that everyone can play.

- Instead of competing for points, change the rules so that the goal is to hit the ball back and forth over the net as many times as possible.

- To guarantee that everyone will be helped to hit the ball, play that everyone on each side must touch the ball before a point is scored.

- Experiment with different kinds of balls instead of a volleyball.

- Playing with a balloon or beach ball lightens the atmosphere.

- Playing with a monster-ball, a weather balloon or with several beach balls in a mesh bag gets several children involved in helping each other throw the ball over the net and hit it back from the other side.

- Having several balls in play at once gives more chances and keeps everyone more alert.

- Use Frisbees, ping pong paddles or badminton racquets as bats or use blankets to toss a beach ball or a large rubber ball back and forth over the net.

- Set up nets in the shape of an X and play four-sided volleyball or play volleyball on a tennis court that has a low net.

- Play with everyone starting out on one side of the net. The first player bats the balloon or ball to another player and runs under the net to the other side. The second player bats the balloon or ball to another player and runs under the net. This goes on until the last person bats the ball over the net and follows it by running under the net. Now that everyone has made it to the other side, go through the same process until everyone ends up on the other side again.

Having several
balls in play
at once gives
more chances
and keeps
everyone
more alert.

Scrub

Scrub or **Work Up** is a pick-up adaptation of baseball that used to be played daily in neighborhood parks throughout Canada and the United States. Up to four people line up to bat and there is an umpire, catcher, pitcher, short stop and people on all three bases. The rest are in the field. The game follows regular softball or slo-pitch rules with underhand pitching and a softer ball. When batters go out, they go out in the field and everyone rotates positions in this order:

- fielders move from right to left field
- far left field goes to third base
- third base goes to second base
- second base goes to first base
- first base goes to short stop
- short stop goes to pitcher
- pitcher goes to back catcher
- back catcher goes to umpire
- umpire goes to batter

(continued on the next page)

LEAVING OUT LOSING

An entire day of cooperative games builds a caring community spirit in a neighborhood, camp, school or other community setting.

(*Scrub* continued)

As in all good games there are many variations to this basic pattern.

- Play in partners with two batters at a time and two pitchers.

- Give inexperienced players more chances by making a rule that they cannot be put out before getting to first base (many strikes are allowed, a hit in any direction is allowed, no tagging until after first base).

- Speed up the rotation by making a rule that players go out into the field once they get back to home base.

- Play **California Kick Ball** by rolling a large rubber ball to the "batter" who kicks it.

- Play **Volley Baseball** by serving a volley ball to the batter who volleys it or catches and throws it.

- Play **Basket Baseball** by replacing the bases with buckets. The pitcher serves a volley ball to the batter who runs around the bases as soon as he or she hits the ball.. The players on the field try to catch the ball and get it into one of the buckets before the runner makes it home.

- Play **Sponge Ball** with a soft spongy ball and a table tennis paddle.

Sticky-Wickets

Set up an obstacle course for the children to go through in partners or small groups. When they finish, they may want to find a different partner and go through all over again. Here are some ideas for obstacle courses.

- **Mini Golf:** Make a home-made mini golf course with the rule that two children hold on to a putter at the same time.

- **Partner Croquet:** Lay out a croquet course with the rule that two children hold on to the mallet at the same time.

- **Hula Hoop And Balloon Course:** Two or three children bat a balloon back and forth while walking. (No holding the balloon under an arm and charging from hoop to hoop.) Every time they come to a hula hoop, they pick the hoop up, bat the balloon through it and put it back down before going on to the next hoop.

- **Playground Obstacle Course:** Make up a route through the playground and add in partner challenges such as going through back to back, holding both hands, with legs tied together or on piggy back.

Cooperative Games Day

An entire day of cooperative games builds a caring community spirit in a neighborhood, camp, school or other community setting. A planning committee mixes children and adults of all different ages, abilities and backgrounds into diverse teams of about fifteen to twenty people. It is important to make sure that each team is headed up by at least one inclusive travel guide who is familiar with the connecting skill of leaving out losing and the ground rules of safety, equality, respect and fun.

In the morning, children and adults share and play a variety of cooperative games in their separate teams. They can borrow supplies from a central store of basic playground equipment, art material and drama props.

In the afternoon, teams have a few minutes to plan a game that will involve all of the teams in one large group. Each team has a turn leading the large group to play their game.

LEAVING
OUT
LOSING

Showing Off

Children love participating in costume parties, dance contests, pet shows, art shows, bake-offs, drama festivals or musical performances. Leave out losing by having enough categories that everyone wins a prize.

Around The World

Take children to the library to read books about games from around the world. Browse through these books and try out some of the games from cooperative cultures that leave out losing. A few of these games will become new favorites.

Laws Of The Jungle

"Survival of the Fittest" is only one of many types of relationships between living beings. Organize a scavenger hunt that explores the many ways that nature has of leaving out losing. Here are some natural laws to search for.

- *Interdependence:* Helping each other out, each needing the other to survive.

- *Cooperation*: Helping each other out without a need to survive.

- *Dependence*: One being needing another in order to survive.

- *Interconnection*: Together in a web of life.

- *Segregation*: Living side by side without any contact with each other.

- *Integration*: One large group welcoming an individual or small group.

- *Interaction*: Equal exchange between living beings.

- *Transformation*: Starting out as one thing and growing into another.

- *Other laws of the jungle:* Encourage children to describe other relationships they notice.

When children come back and share their observations of examples of natural laws they will be teaching each other a great deal about ecology.

Leave out losing by having enough categories that everyone wins a prize.

KEEPING COOL WHEN THINGS GET HOT

> The eensy weensy spider went up the water spout.
> Down came the rain and washed the spider out.
> Out came the sunshine and dried up all the rain.
> Now, eensy weensy spider went up the spout again.
>
> (BRITISH FOLK SONG)

My heart went out to Jake when I came across him so furiously out of control. He looked just like Yosemite Sam, the character from the Bugs Bunny cartoons who jumps up and down in an ineffective rage with steam coming out of his head. The other kids were practically rolling around on the ground in gales of laughter over the scene they had provoked and the poor guy really did look so comical that it was hard not to laugh myself as I motioned the audience of clowns to settle down. When the smoke cleared, Jack was still sputtering. *"It's not fair. They won't stop making fun of my name. They are always calling me Flaky Jake or Jake the Snake or telling me to Jump in the Lake. I hate it when they tease me about my name."*

"Yeah," I replied, *"It's infuriating when kids make up put-downs that rhyme with your own name. Sometimes it's hard to have a name that is easy to match with so many words. That used to happen to me a lot with my last name. The kids would call me 'Over the Hill,' 'Linda the Pill,' and I really hated being called 'Hill-Billy Goat.'"*

"What did you do about it?" asked Jake.

"I learned to take a deep breath and relax, and say to myself, 'It's only a nickname. Lots of kids have nicknames.' And then, when the television show called the Beverly Hillbillies started, I decided that I kind of liked being called 'Hill-Billy Goat.' What nicknames do you have that you like?" I asked.

Jake thought for a moment, "Well, I like it when my Dad calls me Jake the Great."

"Well, I doubt these kids will tease you again, because they understand now that your feelings are hurt, but, if you ever get teased by other kids, you could try to get a picture of your Dad saying 'Jake the Great, Jake the Great' over and over again. If you keep your cool, the kids will think of something more interesting to do in about a minute."

From then on, Jake was able to keep cool about his great name, and the other kids did stop teasing him. Jake and I kept up a game between ourselves for a long time afterward though. Whenever we saw each other, he would call out *"Hi there, Hill Billy!"* and I would call back *"Hey, Jake the Great, how ya doin'?"* It's funny how being laughed at feels so horribly hot and cold, while laughing together feels so comfortably warm and cool.

SKILL 16: KEEPING COOL WHEN THINGS GET HOT

KEEPING COOL WHEN THINGS GET HOT

People who have learned to stay calm under pressure are able to think clearly, accept responsibility, continue to care about others and find ways to make a positive difference even when things get tough.

Keeping cool when things get hot means learning to pay attention to early signs of frustration and then taking constructive action to stay calm and collected.

Here are some constructive actions.

- Learn strategies for relaxing.
- Use communication skills to express frustrations and to suggest changes and adaptations.
- Think thoughts that put the challenge in perspective.
- Take a break.
- Ask for and offer to help.
- Break the problem into smaller pieces.
- Bring in reinforcements by cheering oneself and others on.

Keeping cool when things get hot means learning to pay attention to early signs of frustration and then taking constructive action to stay calm and collected.

*Tip: Giving children structured opportunities to successfully handle frustration makes it more likely that they can stay relaxed in response to the occasional difficulties and disappointments that are a part of everyday life.
They will be able to cope without losing control and without giving up.*

With skilled
guidance from
an adult, this
semi-competitive
game has endless
opportunities
for kids to
practice
keeping cool.

Children can learn to keep cool when things get hot by playing games and participating in activities that are challenging enough to be difficult and frustrating without being impossible or out of control. Puzzles, strategy games and semi-competitive games where children can quickly get another turn are all good activities for practicing keeping cool under pressure.

Square Ball

With skilled guidance from an adult, this semi-competitive game has endless opportunities for kids to practice keeping cool. The square ball court is drawn with chalk on pavement, as shown in this diagram:

The server is in the back corner or just outside the "D" square (sometimes called the **King's Court**). Three more children stand at the back of (or just outside of) the C, B, and A squares. The rest of the children wait their turn by lining up outside the "A" square.

At the start of a round, the server bounces a rubber ball in his own square and then taps it into another child's square. That child lets the ball bounce once (and only once) and then taps it into someone else's square. Although the basic rules are simple, things get hot over and over again because the ball goes out of play often. Whenever the play stops, someone needs to go out. Here are the rules for going out.

- If the ball lands outside the court or on a line, the person who touched the ball last is out.

- If the ball bounces into someone's square and that person misses it after the first bounce, then that person is out.

- If anyone touches the ball with any part of their body, without letting it bounce in their square first, they are out.

The person who goes out joins the back of the line, everyone rotates to fill in the empty square, and the first child in line goes in to the "A" square. As soon as this rotation takes place, the person in the "D" square puts the ball back into play again.

Inclusive leaders make players aware that everyone has more fun when the ball goes back into play quickly. The more cooling strategies there are in play, the more fun **Square Ball** can become.

KEEPING COOL WHEN THINGS GET HOT

- Figure out cool ways for deciding who should go out. Some ideas are negotiating, voting or volunteering to go out.

- Bring in the reinforcements for staying cool. Cheer on children who accept the decision of the group calmly instead of arguing endlessly or stomping off.

- Make a rule that anyone who has been in D square for more than three turns goes to the end of the line to give others a chance.

- Cooperate to help each other keep the ball in play for as many turns as possible. Children in line stay involved by counting bounces. With practice playing **Square Ball** can begin to look and feel like a fast paced gymnastics routine.

- Add rules that give inexperienced players more chances (such as new players can catch the ball, children can't go out until they have advanced to Square B or new players can pick a partner to help).

- Add challenges for more experienced players (such as skilled players hit with their non-dominant hand, stand facing backwards or clap after hitting the ball).

- Add more squares and play **Six Square** or **Eight Square**.

- Draw more courts and have two or more games going on at the same time.

Children build skill and confidence by role-playing constructive ways of handling pressures and challenges.

Cool Role Plays

Children build skill and confidence by role-playing constructive ways of handling pressures and challenges. Role-playing these solutions in a relaxed setting also makes it likely that individual children will remember to use these strategies when they find themselves in hot situations. Videotaping these scenes is an effective coaching strategy and also shows parents, teachers and other adults how much the children they care about are capable of in a supportive setting. Here is a list of some constructive ways of keeping cool when things get hot.

- *Relaxation:* For example taking deep breaths and tensing then relaxing each muscle.

- *Visualization:* Such as getting a picture of being a super-hero who is staying calm.

- *Communication:* One idea is to acknowledge the difficulty by saying something like: "Wow, this is hard!" Another idea is to use "I feel" messages such as "I'm getting frustrated with this one!" A third idea is to ask for help. "I can't do this one alone, I need someone to help me."

(continued on the next page)

KEEPING COOL WHEN THINGS GET HOT

Break the challenge into smaller steps and learn to do one part of the activity.

*(**Cool Role Plays** continued)*

🐱 *Negotiation:* Sometimes it helps to suggest changes: "How about if we change the rules so that two kids are "It" at the same time?" Another possibility is to suggest adaptations and accommodations such as doing things in partners, taking a longer turn, giving more chances before ending a turn or individually adapting the challenge so that each person is trying to do something that is difficult but not impossible.

🐱 *Being philosophical:* Some expressions put the challenge in perspective: "It's only a game, nothing to get upset about." "We've been through tough times before and we'll go through tough times again!"

🐱 *Take a break:* Get a drink of water or count to ten in any language you are just learning. The concentration on counting gives a mental break from the hot situation.

🐱 *Task analysis:* Break the challenge into smaller steps and learn to do one part of the activity. "Could you show me that part about learning to juggle by throwing two balls instead of three?"

🐱 *Bring in the reinforcements:* Cheer others on. "Wow, you sure did that well, Steph." "Nice throw, Jacques." "Hurray for Rada, that was a great effort!" "Go Angie, go Angie, go!"

Choose Your Own Adventure Stories

Children can make up their own multiple choice adventure stories by choosing different solutions to frustrating problems, writing about the consequences of choosing each solution and then jigsawing the stories together. Word processors make this very easy. Here are the steps:

1. First children think of a frustrating problem (for example, something gets broken or lost, someone breaks a promise, someone has an emergency).

2. Next everyone brainstorms possible ways of responding to that problem and selects three or four choices to write about.

3. Now, children get into three or four groups, each group selects a different choice and writes a paragraph about what happened next. Some of the paragraphs will lead naturally to a positive or negative outcome and that adventure will end. Other paragraphs will lead to another choice point.

4. At each choice point children cycle through the same sequence of brainstorming possible solutions, selecting three or four possible choices and then writing separate paragraphs about what happened next after each choice was made.

5. Once all the stories have come to an end, put the stories together, illustrate them, number the pages and direct the reader to turn to the correct page at each choice point.

6. Read your **Choose Your Own Adventure** stories together and to others.

Cool Cartoons

Drawing cartoons is another good way of rehearsing how to stay cool when things get hot. First get a cartooning book out of the library and show children the basic steps in creating cartoon characters with a variety of facial expressions. Then write different things people can say to themselves to keep cool in the talking bubbles above the characters. Display these positive messages on a bulletin board or make photocopies and award them as certificates of recognition for staying cool in difficult situations.

KEEPING COOL WHEN THINGS GET HOT

Games And Puzzles

Games and puzzles that combine chance and strategy such as Parcheesi (Sorry), Snakes and Ladders, Tic Tac Toe, Checkers, Yahtzee, Pick Up Sticks and Card Games fill rainy afternoons with opportunities to practice keeping cool. Staying calm while getting bumped back to the beginning of the board, sliding down a snake, taking a checker-piece off the board or losing at Tic Tac Toe is all part of the game when everyone is supporting everyone else.

Good Sports Around The World

Ideas about being a good sport vary greatly in different cultures, religions and lifestyles. Ask parents to demonstrate games, jokes and contests from their childhood. Find out how children from different cultures keep cool when things get frustrating.

the patience and harmony that fills our natural world provides incredible inspiration for anyone who wants to cool down.

Martial Arts

Children can explore the complex relationships between keeping cool, learning to be a good sport and learning to fight by visiting a martial arts studio and participating in a lesson. Here are some possible questions for the instructor.

- What are the different kinds of martial arts?
- Does learning martial arts teach people to remain calm? Why or why not?
- Does learning martial arts teach children to be more violent? Why or why not?
- Is it possible to learn the art part without the fighting part?
- How do police, firefighters and paramedics learn to keep cool under stress?

Nature Imagery

The patience and harmony that fills our natural world provides incredible inspiration for anyone who wants to cool down. Encourage children to explore nearby natural areas and find safe places to slip away to for some daily alone time.

Search together for examples of how natural areas have responded to stress and disturbance from wind, water, fire, plants, animals, changes in temperature and the pressures of development. Develop descriptions of one or more of these scenes into relaxing guided imagery sequences, using language that evokes emotions of empathy and respect for the life we share with our earth.

After children have practiced a guided imagery scene several times, they will be able to recall these images on their own to help themselves relax and cope with difficulties.

PRACTICING TOLERANCE

Each of us has his or her own uniqueness and so there are times when we argue with each other. These arguments sometimes bring us closer together. They even make us understand the needs of each other.

(RAMON RETWAIT AND JOE TIUCHEIMAL)

My first English word when I first came home to Canada was "snuggle." I knew a lot more words than that but they were in Kreyol. I remember I was surrounded by white people and it felt weird because I was used to being in Haiti where it was very crowded and very small and I was with my own kind. Then I met my Aunt Sal. My Aunt Sal was white and she also had a disability called cerebral palsy. I remember that my first sight of her felt kind of weird and I didn't think of her as a normal person. I couldn't understand anything she said and I still can't so she signs and my mom tells it to me in English. First she taught me how to sign a bit and then she told me that I should learn more about her before I judge her. So then I went to **Operation Track Shoes.** When you get there, you get buddied up with a partner who has some kind of disability and you spend the weekend with him or her. You get a dorm and there is a big parade and a bunch of track and swimming events. And the whole point is for you to make lots of new friends and at the same time learn about people who have disabilities. I learned that "How would I feel if I had a disability and I was made fun of and laughed at?" Now I think that Aunt Sal is a very normal person and even when I didn't think that she was, she was always.

BY FARAH ARMSTRONG, AGE 8

Yorgas had perfected the skill of belching to the point that he could simultaneously drown out whoever was speaking and turn almost everyone else into limply giggling rag dolls. As for me, I found it completely nauseating and almost impossible to ignore. I forced myself to practice tolerance to the best of my ability and I determinedly searched for something else Yorgas was doing that I could like. We were making a **Video** (page 94) and so I focused my complete attention on his considerable acting talents. The energy was high as we developed characters, plot, setting, story-line and took turns acting out the scenes. Wonder of wonder, miracle of miracles, Yorgas's belches receded in importance to me until they became like a faint, barely noticeable drum beat. The following day, after Yorgas watched himself in the video with all the belches edited out, he became a star performer who never bothered to upstage any of us by burping again.

SKILL 17: PRACTICING TOLERANCE

PRACTICING TOLERANCE

Dealing with discord of any kind is always difficult. Avoiding problems does not guarantee that they will go away. Confronting problems does not always solve them. A third choice between these two reflex responses that is much more likely to lead to positive outcomes is being tolerant. Practicing tolerance means steadfastly ignoring something that bothers you while simultaneously practicing these steps.

- Look away from the negatives and attend to the positive aspects of the situation. Shifting your viewpoint is often all that is needed to bring tolerance into focus.

- Bring in the reinforcements to strengthen whatever seems to be working well. Responding to contributions instead of distractions makes it easier to be tolerant because it brings out the best in everyone.

- Learn about the problem. Gathering information builds tolerance by increasing awareness and understanding.

- Search for constructive solutions. Cooperating together to solve problems often transforms intolerance into respect and appreciation.

Shifting your viewpoint is often all that is needed to bring tolerance into focus.

Tip: People who have moved alot, are from blended families, or have grown up in two or more cultures can often provide leadership in the skill of practicing tolerance because they have had many opportunities to explore different points of view.

PRACTICING TOLERANCE

Here are a some cooperative games, creative activities and experiences with nature that give children many opportunities to practice tolerance.

OPPOSITES ATTRACT

This partnering game (also see **Find A Partner** on page 48) encourages children to view the positive aspects of differences. The leader calls out: "Find people who are different _____ (describe a characteristic)." For example, if the leader says "Find people who are different heights," children then search out one or more children who are shorter or taller than they are. When everyone has found at least one person who is different, the leader calls out a different characteristic to search out.

- Find people who are wearing different kinds of shoes.
- Find someone in a different grade than you are in.
- Find someone who likes different sports than you like.
- Find partners who have different talents.
- Find people from different sized families.
- Find a partner who comes from a different town.
- Get in groups of different ages.
- Find people who come from different countries.
- Get in groups of people who can speak different languages.
- Find people who come from different cultures.
- Find people who learn in different ways than you do.

STRAIGHT FACE

Giggling games are hilarious ways of helping children practice the self control required to ignore distractions. No touching is allowed but almost anything else goes.

Giggling games are hilarious ways of helping children practice the self control required to ignore distractions.

- **Turned To Ice:** Everyone tries to stay perfectly frozen, while one player goes from person to person trying to melt them into puddles of laughter.

- **Funny Faces:** Children get into two groups and one group calls someone from the other group over. That person tries to walk past each person on the other side and look them in the eye without laughing. Children who can manage to keep a straight face return to the group they came from. Children who catch the giggles remain with their new group.

- **My Grandmother's Big Red Toe:** Children take turns asking each other questions. The phrase "My grandmother's big red toe" goes at the end of each answer. For example,
  Question: "What did you do yesterday?"
  Answer: "I played soccer and scored a goal with the help of my grandmother's big red toe."
  Anyone who laughs becomes the next question asker.

PRACTICING TOLERANCE

🐛 **What's Funny About Dirty Socks?:** First make up a set of flash cards that have pictures, cartoons and phrases showing silly situations or difficult situations in life. Some examples are: dirty socks, swimming in cold water, chicken pox, writing tests, cold rice pudding, inside out umbrellas, melting snow, a vending machine or telephone that is out of order, a broken down car, an empty jar of peanut butter, leaving your hat behind, missing a bus, losing twenty dollars, sitting on old chewing gum, having a loose tooth or going to a dentist appointment.

Now, children get into partners or small groups, select a flashcard, think up at least a couple of funny sides to each situation and then act these responses out for the rest of the children. The challenge is to get the audience to laugh before the skit ends or before the actors get the giggles themselves.

MUSICAL ROUNDS

Singing rounds, singing in harmony and playing different musical instruments in a band or an orchestra are all great ways of practicing tolerance (so is patting your head while rubbing your stomach!).

🐛 **Row, Row, Row Your Boat** is a simple round:

FIRST GROUP:	SECOND GROUP:
"Row, row, row your boat"	*(Waits and counts)*
"Gently down the stream"	"Row, row, row your boat"
"Merrily, merrily, merrily, merrily"	"Gently down the stream"
"Life is but a dream"	"Merrily, merrily, merrily, merrily"
"Row, row, row your boat"	"Life is but a dream"

Invite musicians from your community to help you learn other rounds.

Singing rounds, singing in harmony and playing different musical instruments in a band or an orchestra are all great ways of practicing tolerance.

CAN'T JUDGE A BOOK BY ITS COVER

This demonstration shows the importance of really getting to know someone instead of making judgments and assumptions based on first impressions. Help children prepare two separate containers in which the contents are different than what is indicated on the outside. They could be:

🐛 two wrapped boxes with money in the plain package and an old banana peel in the attractive package

🐛 two books with the covers exchanged

🐛 two envelopes with the contents exchanged

🐛 two cereal boxes with the contents exchanged

🐛 two cans with the labels exchanged

(continued on the next page)

PRACTICING TOLERANCE

(*Can't Judge A Book By Its Cover* continued)

Children are now ready to present their demonstration to another group of children by going through this script of guided questions.

> *Question 1: (Hold up one container)* "What is inside this _____ (package, box, can, envelope, book)?" *(Accept all guesses by nodding wisely.)*

> *Question 2: (Hold up second container)* "What is inside this (package, box, can, envelope, book)?" *(Accept all guesses by nodding wisely.)*

> *Question 3: (Ask for several volunteers and ask each of them this question one person at a time)* "If you could only have one of these (boxes, cans, envelopes, books), which one would you choose and why?" *(Accept all answers by nodding wisely.)*

> *Question 4: (Ask for volunteers to open each container, show the contents to everyone and ask this question to everyone.)* "What is the message you got from our demonstration?"

> *Question 5:* "What have you learned about getting to know people from this demonstration?"

CROSS-CULTURAL MURAL

This creative exercise is very useful for building tolerance and understanding between children from two or more different groups who have come together for mutual exchange (for example Native and White youth; Deaf and Hearing students; Girls and Boys; Francophones and Anglophones).

this creative exercise is very useful for building tolerance and understanding between children from two or more different groups who have come together for mutual exchange.

1. First the children get into their separate groups. Each group makes a mural of pictures and slogans that explains their group identity (culture). Children try to get well beyond surface stereotypes to present vividly meaningful images of their values, language, history, traditions, codes of conduct, relationships, struggles, dreams, and reasons for being.

2. The completed murals are displayed and each group has one or two minutes to present the highlights of their mural.

3. Children find a partner from the other group and spend a few minutes viewing the murals together. They may ask each other questions, show each other the most important parts or walk back and forth between the murals, looking for similarities and differences between their groups.

4. Children go back to their separate cultural groups and help each other cut their mural up into separate images, like pieces of a jigsaw puzzle.

5. Then, everyone from both groups works together to reorganize the pieces into one large jointly created collage. The unique characteristics of one group go on the left hand side. The unique characteristics of the other group go on the right hand side and the shared characteristics go in the middle.

6. Children gather together in a circle and take turns saying what they learned from making this cross-cultural collage.

DIFFERENT FOOD

Although many children suffer from allergies, many more children reject different foods simply because they are unfamiliar. There are many ways to encourage children to try different kinds of foods from around the world.

- ᕙ Invite families to a potluck meal (each family brings a dish of food to share).

- ᕙ Invite people from different countries to demonstrate how to make different kinds of food.

- ᕙ Get books out of the library, select recipes and try to make different types of foods.

- ᕙ Go to a multi-cultural food fair. Set a price limit and ask each child to order something they have never tasted before for everyone to share.

- ᕙ Visit several different kinds of grocery stores. (Let the managers know that your purpose is to sample different kinds of food.) Purchase one type of food from each place that none of you have ever tasted before and take it to a park for a picnic.

PEACE ART

Millions of people around the world are communicating messages of tolerance and understanding through visual arts such as drawing, painting, sculpture and photography, as well as expressive arts such as dance, music and drama. There are many ways to get involved.

- ᕙ Take children to watch musicians, dancers, artists and actors who are exploring issues related to multi-culturalism, diversity, anti-racism and peace building.

- ᕙ Invite artists from different backgrounds to help you get children involved in exploring diversity through art, music, dance and drama.

- ᕙ Have a movie festival about peaceful leaders throughout world history.

- ᕙ Go to the library and find books, videos and CDs that promote peace through drama, music and art.

- ᕙ Go out with a camera and take pictures of all the peace art you can find.

SLUGS, SPIDERS AND SNAKES

Learning about some of the less popular beings on the planet builds understanding and tolerance by reducing prejudice. With guidance to become careful observers, most children find watching slugs, worms, ants, tadpoles and other smaller creatures of the oceans, ponds, fields and woods to be much more fascinating than trying to make each other scream by throwing helpless beings around. Children can learn most about these animals by watching them in the wild areas where they live. A knowledgeable naturalist or biologist can add background information.

Learning about some of the less popular beings on the planet builds understanding and tolerance by reducing prejudice.

NO-GO-TELL

When Matt Dolmage was born with so many differences, his mom, Marilyn, received more cards expressing sympathy than congratulations. Friends, relatives, people at work and people at church all took their turn suggesting that Matt and his family would be better off if they could leave him in a hospital and get on with their lives. The Dolmages said "No" to these pressures. They went and searched for help from people involved in building inclusive communities and they have supported him to grow up in the center of a loving circle of family and friends. Matt and his family have now been guiding neighborhoods, schools, camps, and government on inclusive explorations for over twenty-six years. One of Matt's gifts is the ability to connect people together through music. Jam sessions at home with Matt on the electric piano, Dad on the fiddle, brother Jay composing the words, friends playing guitars and bongo drums and sister Leah on the spoons are quite an experience that couldn't be happening if Matt had been excluded from his family.

NO-GO-TELL

The giant's garden
Is up there on the hill-top
Where he looks down
On children who tease others.

The giant has a long stick
He carries around
Looking for teasers
To put in his sack

(LULLABY SUNG TO CHILDREN WHO ARE
FOND OF TEASING OR BULLYING OTHERS.
ROVIANA, SOLOMON ISLANDS)

"We have a rule against putting people down in our school, but it isn't commonly followed. Grant is a boy in my class who often gets teased by lots and lots of kids because he is disabled in some ways and he can't do some of the things that other people do. It's strange because even though he's one of the best soccer players in the school no one passes him the ball when they play. So, my friend and I started playing soccer with him when he had no one to play with, which was most of the time. When we played together, the other kids sometimes said nasty things to us like 'Oh my God, they are going to play with Grant.' Finally, we went and told the duty supervisor and she helped us to stand up for ourselves. We told people not to tease him or pick on him and we told them to 'Treat us like you would treat yourself.' We tell ourselves that we can be friends with whoever we want whether we get teased or not. Grant is really nice and he's been teaching us a lot. Now soccer has become my favorite thing to do."

BY JADE, AGE 9

by Danika Carlson, age 6

SKILL 18: NO-GO-TELL

NO-GO-TELL

Risks are part of daily life including all human relationships and all social, leisure, recreational, educational and work activities. It is important for children to learn to recognize dangerous situations where there is a high risk of physical, mental or emotional harm to self or others and take actions to be safe and get help if needed.

The three basic steps are to say "No", leave the situation and get help from safe, competent people such as parents, teachers, police and other emergency responders. Children who have No-Go-Tell skills are able to take these types of actions.

the three basic steps are to say "No", leave the situation and get help.

- Take steps to prevent accidents.
- Stand up to social pressure or bullying.
- Avoid or leave situations that seem dangerous.
- Respond effectively to emergencies.
- Get help when needed.

 A strong word of caution: The children's nursery rhyme, "sticks and stones may break my bones, but words can never hurt me" is a myth. On-going teasing, put downs, or threats can cause fear, anger and illness as well as low self esteem. Encourage children to use **No-Go-Tell** skills to put a stop to verbal, physical or sexual harrassment.

NO-GO-TELL

Here are several cooperative games, creative activities and experiences in nature that give children enjoyable and interesting opportunities to practice the steps of No-Go-Tell.

Run Away Games

There are several traditional children's games that specifically teach the skill of turning around and running away from danger. Here are two examples.

- **What Time Is It Mr. Wolf?:** Children line up at one end of the room or outdoor area and walk toward a wolf at the other end asking: "What time is it Mr. Wolf". If the wolf answers with a time such as "9:00" or "6:00" it is safe to keep walking forward. If the wolf answers with a meal such as "lunch time" or "snack time," everyone runs back home, while the wolf chases behind and tries to tag someone and turn them into the next wolf.

- **Watch Out For The Monster:** Children line up at one end of the room or outdoor area and walk toward a monster at the other end asking: "What are you doing _____ (name of the monster)? If the monster answers with an activity such as "cleaning my house," "watching television," or "digging in the garden" it is safe to keep walking forward. But if the monster answers "Gobbling you up!" everyone runs back home, trying not to be tagged. The child who gets tagged is turned into the next monster.

No-Go-Tell Awards

This activity acknowledges people who have stood up for themselves and others. Ask children to use the following list to find people to interview and nominate for the **No-Go-Tell Awards**. Interview someone who:

- prevented an accident
- stood up for a person, an animal or a natural area
- said "No" to a dangerous situation
- got away from danger
- went and got help to solve a dangerous situation

Hold an awards ceremony and present certificates honouring aspects of applying No-Go-Tell skills.

No-Go-Tell Videos

Help children find videos about people who have used the skills of No-Go-Tell. Some examples from National Film Board of Canada to get you started are:

- *For Angela*
- Playing Fair Series (*Walker, Hey Kelly, Mela's Lunch, Carol's Mirror*)

These videos show children how to stand up and say "No" to racism and other potentially dangerous situations. They show how to go and get help if needed. Remember that the dialogue after is the most important part of watching videos.

Remember that the dialogue after is the most important part of watching videos.

Dramatic Problem Solving

 Solving Scary Situations: Children pick a card with a scary situation on it and make up skits that show the No-Go-Tell steps. Some examples are:

- falling out of a boat or being in deep water
- being pressured to smoke or steal
- being tricked into touching or being touched on a private area of the body
- being picked on, harassed or bullied
- smelling smoke
- getting lost
- being with someone who is driving too fast
- getting money or possessions stolen
- watching a video that turns out to be really upsetting or scary
- being followed by someone
- another child being called names or getting chased
- finding an envelope with money in it
- being caught in a snowstorm

 Stop-Action Drama: Children act out the beginning of a problem situation, such as one of the scary situations from the list above. When things start going wrong, someone calls out "Stop!". Children offer suggestions for handling the situation more successfully and the actors act out the suggestions.

Any reasonable solution is a right answer and children can help each other.

🦈 **Crossing the River:** Everyone lines up on one side of the river. One or two at a time, they approach the boat owner who is willing to paddle them across the river on one condition: They need to solve a **Scary Situation** first by sharing the No-Go-Tell steps. Any reasonable solution is a right answer and children can help each other.

No-Go-Tell Stories

People from all cultures tell **No-Go-Tell Stories** to help children learn to think about how to avoid or get out of dangerous situations. These are true and fictional stories in which the main character:

🦈 prevents something dangerous from happening

🦈 gets away or helps others get away from danger

🦈 stands up for people or animals

🦈 tells the truth

🦈 acts like a hero

🦈 gets help

(continued on the next page)

It is always fascinating to compare the dangers that children growing up in different environments are taught to avoid.

(*No-Go-Tell Stories* continued)

There are many sources of **No-Go-Tell Stories**. Here are three ideas.

- Read myths, fairy tales, and hero stories from around the world.
- Listen to parents tell No-Go-Tell Stories from their childhood.
- Watch for No-Go-Tell Stories in the news and keep a collection of newspaper clippings.

It is always fascinating to compare the dangers that children growing up in different environments are taught to avoid. For example, the biggest dangers in the Arctic are freezing to death or falling through the ice and so there are many, many Inuit No-Go-Tell Stories that warn children about these dangers.

Safety and Survival Skills

Children can learn how to prevent, prepare for, and respond to emergencies and disasters such as:

- earthquakes, fires, floods and other natural disasters
- health emergencies such as choking, heart attacks or allergic reactions
- car accidents
- other accidents — such as getting lost, falling, eating poison, getting a cut, an animal bite or a bee sting

There are many safety courses and drills for children such as First Aid, Emergency Responding, Water Safety, Safety in the Woods, Street Proofing, Baby Sitter Training, and Fire Drills. There are also many books about safety and survival for parents and other adults to read along with children.

Saying No to Television, Videos and Computer Games

In addition to all the good they offer; television, video games, and computers contain many dangers. Teach children how to make safe choices and how to use No-Go-Tell strategies to get away from shows, video games, or computer activities they don't want to watch or play. Many children are relieved to learn that they have the right to prevent nightmares by not watching disturbing movies, television shows and videos or not playing the violent computer games that are being so heavily marketed.

- Teach children to change the channel, turn off the television or computer, hide their eyes and/or leave the room if they don't like what is on the screen.
- Together, make a list of safe and enjoyable shows to watch, games to play and web sites to visit.
- Ask babysitters and older siblings to help make sure younger children do not watch scary shows.

Self Defense

NO-GO-TELL

Bring an expert such as the police, a self-defense instructor, a street worker or a crisis line worker to help children develop self defense skills. Contrary to popular belief, fighting back is not the most effective self-defense strategy because it usually increases the danger. Preventing danger is the best defense. Getting away to safety is second best. Fighting to get away is the third last resort. Here are some examples of effective self defense strategies.

- Go places together instead of walking places alone.
- Pay attention to early feelings of discomfort or other warning signs.
- Hang around with people who can be trusted.
- Keep busy doing things that are fun and safe.
- Teach children to tell themselves over and over again that they are "VIPs" (Very Important People) who have the right to be safe.
- Avoid cigarettes, alcohol, drugs, exploitative sex, hitch-hiking and other health hazards.
- Help someone who is in trouble to get to a safe place.
- Go to get help for someone who seems to be in trouble.
- Walk away from problems by walking toward safe places and people.

teach children how to make safe choices.

Stop Posters

Children can get out their art supplies and make posters that show positive No-Go-Tell alternatives to various dangers such as discrimination, drugs, accidents or pollution. Get permission to display them in the window of a local store or another public place in your community.

Standing Up For Nature

Since the natural world communicates in ways other than speech, naturalists and environmentalists are people who have learned to speak out on Nature's behalf. Introduce children to the many people in your community who have stood up to protect parks, heritage sites, sacred spots, sensitive ecological areas and other special places on Earth. Visit the natural areas in your community that have been protected and looked after.

CHALLENGE
BY CHOICE

I once spent a weekend learning about **Adventure Programming** (see page 137) with about two hundred camp counsellors. These teenagers and young adults had all grown up spending every summer at camp since about the age of about six. They were each shining with the imaginative leadership skills they had developed through play. They could make up fantastical stories, silly skits and hilarious jokes at the drop of a hat. They organized games, drama, hikes, picnics, nature walks, swimming, music, camp fires, star parties and other adventures at a pace that kept us going from sun-up until well after midnight. There was very little time or need to read, listen to lectures or write reports during this learning experience. We learned about 'challenge by choice' by challenging ourselves. We learned how to 'leave out losing' by making sure that every single person could take part in every single activity. We learned about 'inventing possibilities' by mixing and matching ideas to develop brand new activities that had never been done before and may never be done in quite that way again. The abilities these young leaders had to handle every situation with laughter, and their abilities to figure out enjoyable ways to include me and everyone else in absolutely everything was an incredible, unforgettable experience of a life time. The joy and inclusion I experienced going back to summer camp at age forty-five gave me great hope for children of the new millennium.

I CHALLENGE MYSELF TO:

Sing on the street and not just in the shower
Swim against the flow
Wear a shirt that doesn't match my pants
Dance to the beat of a different drummer
Eat my ice cream cone from the bottom to the top
Sail on calm days
Be a square peg in a round hole
Laugh by myself
Run the race backwards
Talk my own language
Play in the rain
Think out of the box
Duck under the high jump bar
Ask two kids to be my partners
Choose to be
        as different as I want to be!

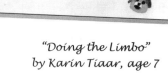

*"Doing the Limbo"
by Karin Tiaar, age 7*

SKILL 19: CHALLENGE BY CHOICE

CHALLENGE BY CHOICE

Sharing imaginative, confident adventures are what challenge by choice is all about. Children who dare to have adventures develop self esteem, skills, strength, creativity and energy. Children who dare to bridge differences by taking adventures together develop relationships that are solidly caring and boldly joyful.

An inclusive group creates a safety-net of trust and mutual support so that children can build confidence to meet their own personal challenges as well as challenges everyone in the group agrees to try.

Inclusive groups set individual and collective goals and challenges. Respect for choice keeps peer pressure out of the picture. Everyone helps everyone else to do what they have decided to do.

An inclusive group creates a safety-net of trust and mutual support so that children can build confidence.

- Many challenges are done in partners and small groups. In challenge by choice, it is perfectly OK for the people who are more skilled to help the others to succeed.

- Instead of comparing themselves to others, children measure their success in terms of their own goals.

- The challenges are made fun by using the powers of everyone's imaginations and the wonders of the outdoors to enhance perceived risks while controlling the actual risk.

Tip: One choice at a time, group members encourage each person to set realistic, measurable, individual goals that are at the edges of, but not outside of, what is possible (and in our imaginations, everything is possible).

Here are some games and activities that give children adventurous opportunities to choose individual and group challenges.

HOPSCOTCH

Hopscotch is one of many traditional games where the more skilled players have opportunities to try out very challenging moves, while the beginning players are working on simpler tricks. Hopscotch is played on a court drawn with chalk (on pavement) or a stick (on dirt or sand). One of the classic courts looks like this, but there are many variations:

More skilled players have opportunities to try out very challenging moves, while the beginning players are working on simpler tricks.

Children take turns throwing an object into one of the squares and then jumping from one square to another. Their turn ends when they step on a line, lose their balance, jump in a square that has a stone in it or throw their object out of bounds.

The turns are kept approximately the same length by varying what each child throws, how far away each child stands before they make the throw and by varying how each child moves around the court (hopping, jumping or any other way). Children can also play hopscotch in partners with one throwing and one jumping.

SKIPPING GAMES

With two children turning the rope and everyone else in line, you are ready for skipping challenges. Children can try individual tricks or they can jump in twos, threes, fours or however many can fit in the rope. Here are a few examples from very easy to almost impossible!

- **Sticks, Swings, and Snakes:** Children jump over a still rope, a swinging rope, or a wriggling rope that is being held at different heights.

- **Run Through the Door:** Children run through the rope as it is turning overhand. The back door is much harder than the front door.

- **Skipping Rhymes:** There are thousands of poems, counting rhymes and action rhymes that kids have made up over as many years. Here's one: "Gymnastic spiders do the splits, Spanish dancers do high kicks, Kangaroos spin right around, I'm done jumping so I'll leave town!" (run out of the rope)

🎋 **Elastic Skipping Ropes:** Children from parts of China, Japan and Switzerland make skipping ropes out of elastic and perform jumping tricks while two children hold the elastic. Beginning at ankle level, the height is increased each time a trick is performed successfully. Some games use a single strand held by one leg or one hand. Other games use a double strand that goes around both legs.

🎋 **Double Dutch:** The turners turn two ropes toward each other, in an even alternate rhythm (this is almost as hard as jumping!). The jumper jumps both ropes.

🎋 **Games From The Attic:** Children can learn more skipping games from older children, parents, the library and now on the Internet.

WATER CHALLENGES

When skilled life-guarding, buddy systems and other safety precautions are in place, the challenges of playing in, on and above the water provide endless fun.

the challenges of playing in, on and above the water provide endless fun.

🎋 **Water Tricks:** Perform tricks such as somersaults, hand stands, dives and acrobatic stunts.

🎋 **Water Animals:** Pretend to be animals such as jellyfish, barnacles, salmon, dolphins, seals and otters.

🎋 **Line Up:** Weave back and forth, in and out, or over and under legs and arms.

🎋 **Take Aim:** Throw water balloons and play with water squirters.

🎋 **Candlelight Sail Past:** Make boats, light candles on them and pilot them on a route through the water until the last candle goes out.

🎋 **Make Waves:** Cooperate together to make whirlpools, waves and currents.

🎋 **Water Polo:** Float on inner tubes, air mattresses or kick boards and play water sports.

🎋 **Boating:** Nothing is so much fun as messing about in boats. Skilled, certified and experienced adults and young adults can take children rowing, canoeing, rafting or sailing. Children can make their own rafts and toy boats.

 Caution: Make sure someone is a qualified life guard, everyone has a buddy and that there is a high ratio of adults to children during these water challenges because being on the water really does contain many, many risks in the midst of so much fun.

Nothing is so much fun as messing about in water!

CHALLENGE BY CHOICE

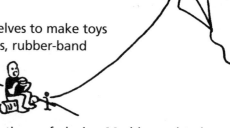

CHALLENGING TOYS

Children through history have challenged themselves to make toys that go faster and farther such as paper airplanes, rubber-band powered boats, sail boats, kites and balloon powered jets. Children also love challenging the forces of gravity and their own dexterity by making and playing with spinning tops, bouncing balls, yo-yos, Frisbees or the ancient pastimes of playing Marbles and Jacks (Knucklebones). Invite older children and parents to demonstrate tricks they have learned. Encourage children to practice and experiment as they set their own challenges and invent new tricks. Contributing materials, helping each other make toys and sharing toys are all part of the challenge.

SPOT DANCE CHALLENGE

Put on some music, dim the lights, get a flashlight and you are ready for a spot dance challenge. At the beginning of a song, the person holding the flashlight calls out a dance such as: the Twist, a Limbo Dance, Chicken Dancing, Lip Synching, Hula, Creative Dance, Jazz Dance, Choose Your Own Dance or any other type of dance.

Invite older children and parents to demonstrate tricks they have learned.

- When the music starts, everyone dances until the beam of the flashlight shines steadily on one of the incredible dancers.

- The incredible dancer now gets a turn to hold the flashlight, select a song, call out a challenge.

- Choosing to respond to a creative challenge is comfortable and fun when there is so much choice, when everyone is cheering each other on and when everyone has a chance to be a creative winner.

- Make videos of your spot-dance challenges.

ART CHALLENGES

Children love getting into small groups and challenging themselves to create drama, art or music. Making videos to commemorate these events is always a lot of fun. Some possible art challenges are:

- make sculptures, murals, kites or forts

- perform skits and pantomimes

- bring in a bunch of props and costumes and improvise a play

- create and perform a musical stage production complete with songs, dance, drama and costumes and linked together by a story-line

Everyone can get involved and contribute in some way — no prior experience needed and showing off talents is encouraged.

MAGIC SHOW

Performing magic tricks for each other is as easy as hocus pocus. Children can learn magic tricks from home, books, videos and from generous magicians.

- Magic tricks can be very simple or very, very difficult.
- They can be done singly or in partners or small groups.
- They can be performed live or on videotape (such as the famous disappearing and reappearing video star).
- Children can work individually, in pairs or in small groups.

Once each child has at least one magic trick or a part in a magic trick, the show can begin. Magic shows present constant challenges: distracting the audience, performing a trick, being a volunteer, watching carefully, guessing how the trick is done and being the clown in between acts.

REDISCOVERING ADVENTURE!

More and more people in communities throughout the world are getting training and experience in **Adventure Programming**, **Rediscovery Camping** and **Experiential Outdoor Education**. Challenge by choice initiatives are often a big part of their training. Obstacle courses, climbing towers, low ropes courses, high ropes courses and climbing walls set the stage for getting everyone involved in supporting each other to safely make more and more challenging choices. These person-made adventures all lead up to choosing natural outdoor challenges such as climbing mountains, exploring rivers and oceans or going caving. For more information see the Resources Section, page 156.

NATURE EXPEDITIONS

With help from one or more experienced leaders, children can head out to explore challenges in the inter-tidal zone, the swamp, the river, the mountains, the woods or the night sky and then report back on their discoveries.

Children can learn magic tricks from home, books, videos and from generous magicians.

INVENTING NEW POSSIBILITIES

Stone Soup

The harvest was poor, the winter was long and everyone in the village was hungry. In one family, the cupboards were bare and there was nothing left in the cellar but a few stones. *"It's stone soup tonight then,"* said Mother. She bid the children to fetch their largest cooking pot. They filled it with water from the village well, and carried it to the village square where Father kindled a blazing fire. Mother washed the stones and dropped them into the water along with some salt and chili pepper. Smelling the aroma of the spices, the neighbors began to gather round. *"Bring your bowls,"* called mother. *"I'm making enough soup for everyone."* The family's generosity in the midst of such hard times warmed everyone. When they brought back their bowls, they also managed to bring a few remaining beans, withered carrots, chicken bones, some old potatoes, the heart of a cabbage, an ear of corn, and even a few tomatoes that had been dried in the sun the past summer. As the gifts were added to the bubbling soup, delicious aromas blended together. When it came time to eat, everyone in the village agreed that such a soup had never been served before. *"Imagine that such a wonderful soup was made from a few stones."*

(A CHILEAN FOLK TALE)

WHAT IS IT, MRS. B?

The Computer Graphics students each had varying technical abilities, not to mention different ages, cultures and genders. A mystery project brought them together while reinforcing the class philosophy of thinking "outside the box."

Each student received a different file containing a puzzle piece template, along with instructions to go on an online scavenger hunt to collect images that captured their individual perceptions of current events and trends (both likes and dislikes).

It was wonderful to see the teens compare ideas and help each other find what they needed. As a group, they were overcoming the stereotype that computer work is a solitary activity.

Once their collages were prepared, students followed a chart to apply colors to the drawn shapes within each piece. At this point some of the students began guessing what the result would be once the images were pieced together by the instructor.

On the day of the unveiling, they were delighted to see that they had made a gigantic sandwich (complete with flies!) with the caption, "Reality is a sandwich I did not order" imprinted on the olive garnish on top.

BY KIM BARNARD

SKILL 20: INVENTING NEW POSSIBILITIES

INVENTING NEW POSSIBILITIES

Divergent thinking is a wonderful skill for inventing new ways of being together in our increasingly diverse world. When different ideas are combined together in new ways it becomes easy to creatively solve problems, get around barriers and find more ways of celebrating everyone's different gifts.

Two or more heads are always better than one when it comes to combining different ideas together. Everyone can get involved.

- ☆ Bring two or more different points of view together to invent new games, activities, contraptions and experiences.

- ☆ Analyze goals and look for different ways of getting to the same destination.

- ☆ Combine different gifts and talents together to come up with new ways of doing old things.

- ☆ Think of alternative ways for individuals to get actively involved.

- ☆ Break activities and problems into small steps and work together on coming up with new ways of doing each step.

Combine different gifts and talents together to come up with new ways of doing old things.

Tip: *Laughing and learning together will lead children toward new possibilities that are creative and enjoyable celebrations of everyone's different contributions.*

INVENTING
NEW
POSSIBILITIES

Here are some ideas for getting everyone involved in inventing new possibilities together. Notice how the capital letters in the titles of the activities in this section have been invented by combining letters and tools together.

Inventing Adaptations

There is no need to give up on an activity that seems too difficult, uncomfortable, inconvenient, expensive, culturally inappropriate or any other problem. There is also no need to give up and leave children out who don't easily fit into certain activities. Games, activities and nature experiences can always be adapted in ways that accommodate the needs of individual children. Often the process of figuring out accommodations leads children to discover or invent brand new games and activities that are even more enjoyable than the original idea. Any of the activities in this book can be adapted or transformed into a new possibility.

Here are some examples of how various sports have been adapted to accommodate different disabilities. Borrow video tapes or ask members of various disability sports associations to demonstrate and then get children directly involved in experiencing the challenges of these adapted sports.

Games, activities, and nature experiences can always be adapted in ways that accommodate the needs of individual children.

☆ **Goal Ball:** The sighted players wear blindfolds in this fast-paced echo-location game using a ball that makes sounds as it moves.

☆ **Wheelchair Sports:** In just-for-fun games, the challenges are equalized by giving everyone a wheelchair. In high level competitions, the challenges are equalized by complex handicapping systems based on level of disability.

☆ **Football Huddle:** Deaf football players at Gallaudet University for the Deaf in Washington, DC invented the football huddle so that no one could see their signing when they discussed strategies.

☆ **Disabled Sailing:** Sam Sullivan, the same man who invented all terrain wheelchairs for hiking (see page 45), has helped oceans and lakes become accessible to sailors who have disabilities. "On the water you leave your wheelchairs and the challenges of everyday living behind."

☆ **Let It Snow:** Inventive ingenuity has been applied out on the slopes to figure out hundreds of ways that children with any type of disability or ability can get involved in skiing.

☆ **Horseback Riding:** Riding a horse builds up self esteem at the same time that children are exercising every muscle in their bodies and experiencing the power of guiding a horse in the ring and out on the trail. More than 600 therapeutic riding associations across North America have figured out endless ways to accommodate children with various disabilities.

Prop Boxes

Every inventor needs several boxes of materials and props. Get children involved in collecting the contents of these boxes.

INVENTING NEW POSSIBILITIES

☆ **Scientist's Box:** Collect broken appliances, rubber bands, the old egg beater, paper clips and other junk.

☆ **Arts and Crafts Box:** You will need a big box for scraps of paper, cardboard, crayons, felts, a stapler, scissors, a hole puncher, tape, glue, paint, socks, wool, needle and thread, tape, paper plates, toilet paper tubes, egg cartons, fabric, feathers, corks, a stamp pad, pipe cleaners, popsicle sticks and other recycled left-overs.

☆ **Drama Box:** Gather masks, old jewelry, old shoes, hats, scarves, costumes, wigs, eye glasses, uniforms, make-up, false teeth, fake tattoos and a pirate's eye patch.

☆ **Building Box:** Children can build many projects with adult supervision if they have access to a hammer, nails, saw, drill, screw driver, pulley, rope, wood and other tools and equipment.

☆ **Exploring Box:** Keep these items in a backpack: flashlight, magnifying glass, jars, buckets, compass, stethoscope, binoculars, telescope and nature identification books.

☆ **Gardening Box:** Children can grow along with the plants. Keep gloves, spade, hoe, watering can, pruning shears, seeds, plants and pots handy.

☆ **Musician's Box:** Keep a box full of sound by collecting a ukulele, bells, rattles, spoons, whistles, horns, sticks, drums and other instruments.

☆ **Culture** and **Time Capsules:** Collect photographs, newspaper articles, scrap books, letters, memorabilia, biographies and artifacts from different cultures and different times in history.

What If?

When children are pretending, there is no limit to the possibilities they can dream up. Without even leaving the room children can:

☆ go camping in any ecosystem in the world

☆ fly to any country in the world, any planet in the solar system or any star in the universe

☆ explore inside the hottest volcano, the deepest ocean or the darkest cave

☆ go on a journey to the center of any forest, the top of any mountain or the heart of any community

When children are pretending, there is no limit to the possibilities they can dream up.

There are many different ways of going on imaginary adventures such as:

☆ playing with dolls and sets of miniature characters and props

☆ story telling and guided imagery

☆ improvisational and scripted drama activities

☆ drawing, writing, singing and other expressive arts

INVENTING
NEW
POSSIBILITIES

Different Drummer Story Telling

Children learn a lot from listening to and telling stories about times people invented ways to solve access barriers. Many popular science fiction and fantasy stories were invented by people who faced tremendous barriers in their real lives. Children can explore stories from:

☆ their own true life experiences

☆ the library

☆ parents, teachers, travellers, entertainers, public speakers, next door neighbors and each other

Access Check

Guide children to take tours of their homes, schools, camps or neighborhoods to check out how well the community is meeting the challenge of inventing new possibilities for people who have various kinds of differences. Children can also interview parents, principals, camp directors, owners of businesses and administrators of organizations to learn about access policies and practices. Look for the following indicators of access.

☆ The presence of ramps, elevators, Braille signs and auditory signalling systems show mobility and vision access.

☆ Signs showing what languages are spoken show an awareness of communication access needs.

☆ The availability of an **Access Guidebook** shows that a community is putting effort into welcoming everyone.

☆ Providing text in alternative formats such as on tape, on a computer disk or translated into different languages (including plain language) shows a willingness to accommodate different ways of accessing printed information.

Write thank you
letters or
give certificates
of commendation
to places and
people who are
taking steps to
welcome people.

☆ The presence of people who are friendly, approachable and willing to make everyone feel welcome is the best sign of good access.

Children can write thank you letters or give certificates of commendation to places and people who are taking steps to welcome people from diverse backgrounds by inventing ways of being more accessible. Also see **Access Walk** (page 45).

PATHS, MAPS and Circles of Friends

Take time to explore these collaborative dreaming, planning and on-going support processes that gather circles of family, friends and other supporters around specific individuals. So much is possible when people share their dreams and solve problems in a hopeful atmosphere of acceptance, valuing and loving creativity. Books, videos and training sessions about these processes are available through **Inclusion Press** (listed in the Resource Section, page 156).

Autobiographies

Reflecting on personal experiences with differences is a great way of learning more about the skill of inventing possibilities. Here are some questions that guide children and adults to explore their personal histories.

☆ What are some of your own differences?

☆ Which differences were/are celebrated as gifts?

☆ Which differences were/are viewed as problems to be fixed?

☆ What are some of your most important memories of exploring diversity?

☆ Who are some inclusive travel guides who influenced you and what possibilities did they invent?

☆ What are some of the lessons you have learned from your personal experience about building bridges across differences?

☆ What are some possibilities that you have invented for yourself or others?

Guide children to invent creative ways of communicating autobiographies through writing, acting and art.

Conservation and Land Stewardship

Guide children to get involved in new possibilities for protecting and caring for the natural places in your community. Many children are learning to leave only footprints and take only photographs in *Junior Naturalist* programs. Other children are participating in building new trails by joining the *Rails to Trails* movement in Canada, the United States and England. Other children are becoming stream keepers, shoreline monitors, land stewards and earth keepers. Many children and their families are getting involved in reducing consumption, reusing materials, recycling leftovers, composting food and everything else that is organic, and conserving water. Other children are becoming bee keepers, gardeners and feeders of wintering birds. More and more schools, camps and parks are getting children involved in planting indigenous plants, tending school gardens, mapping and caring for surrounding wooded areas and even reclaiming streams that had been paved over.

One of the many pleasant outcomes of these projects is that caring for school property has been found to markedly reduce vandalism. The more we learn about valuing people's differences, the more we are learning to value the diversity of all living beings on the planet.

Celebrating

Plan a party, a talent show, a pot luck meal, a children's festival or any special event that will celebrate the time you have spent building bridges across your differences.

INVENTING NEW POSSIBILITIES

So much is possible when people share their dreams and solve problems in a hopeful atmosphere of acceptance, valuing and loving creativity.

Unity Is

To work as one, but realize we are not one.

*To be treated as equals and be admired for our differences,
not neglected for them.*

To work as a team to make sure war, poverty and all feuds are ended.

This is what unity is.

To accept people's beliefs and to never force your own beliefs on them.

To never look at someone differently because of their background.

To understand that no one's opinion is the same and to listen to all sides.

This is what unity is.

*Unity is not the forming of one race. It is the force of all sides using different talents.
War is caused by one race pushing their beliefs onto another trying to become one.
No two people are alike. All values are different. No one person can stop a war,
but everyone working as a team can.*

*We must soon realize that everyone has something to offer and to look within
and find it and bring it out in him or her. Giving someone a more united feeling
makes us all feel more like equals. This will ensure that no one person will feel
less valued than anyone else.*

This is what unity is.

BY AARON HENRY, AGE 13, WINNER OF THE 1999 UNITY ESSAY CONTEST
SPONSORED BY THE VICTORIA CITY POLICE, VICTORIA, BC, CANADA

Part 3:

Creating Inclusive Culture

Inclusive Pioneers

We are fortunate to be living in a time in history when children are being actively encouraged and supported to explore and celebrate diversity. Only forty years ago, when I was a little girl, excluding other children who couldn't easily fit in was an accepted way of life.

My elementary school had two stairways leading up to two separate entrances. Foot high letters inscribed into the stonework showed that one entrance was for BOYS and one entrance was for GIRLS. We had separate play areas too and trespassing was punished with detentions. No wonder the boys were always yelling "Girl Germs" and "Flea Bags" at us.

In First Grade, my next door neighbor was sent away to a different school because she learned too slowly. In Third Grade I was sent away to another different school because I learned too quickly. These experiences with segregation had a powerful influence on my search for alternative ways of dealing with differences.

When a new girl from Germany moved into our neighborhood, I invited her to Brownies. Unfortunately, neither I or my Brownie leaders had a clue about how to welcome someone from another country into a room filled with girls with uniforms, special hand shakes, badges, Brown Owls and a toad stool "piggy bank" that we danced around and dropped money into. I didn't quite realize how badly things had gone wrong until I knocked on her door the next week to invite her to come again. Her mother opened the door a crack, shoved a five-dollar bill into my hand and slammed it shut again. When their family moved away a couple of weeks later I felt as if I had caused them to leave.

Every day our school bus drove past the Native kids who were waiting for their bus to go to the Indian School across town. Aboriginal students in BC who lived on Reserves were not allowed to attend public school until the late 1960s.

What is the age of the woman in this picture? Two opposite answers are possible because the foreground and background switch back and forth between a very elderly woman looking down into the disappointments of the past and a young woman looking over her right shoulder toward a hopeful future. Martin Luther King Jr. once explained this paradox: **"As my suffering mounted I soon realized that there were two ways I could respond to my situation — either to react with bitterness or seek to transform the suffering into a creative force."** His dreams of new possibilities guided millions of people to begin a long journey away from exclusion, toward inclusion.

Each positive and peaceful step one of us takes in an inclusive direction shows the way for many other people who are looking for hope and leadership as we discover how to create inclusive culture together.

An inclusive guide from my childhood

Learning to welcome just one type of difference is a seed that allows awareness of diversity to blossom like flowers in a garden. I was fortunate to have an aunt who sowed many such seeds during her lifetime. It wasn't until I came across her book in a library in 1988 that I realized what a strong influence Aunty Bette had on me.

Bette Hood was a community volunteer, a gifted teacher, a mother of five children, and an aunt of many more. One of many fascinating differences about Aunty Bette was that she had one leg shorter than the other as a result of an encounter with polio when she was a little girl. I think her experience with being physically different was probably a big influence on her belief in *"the dignity of all people."* She was deeply concerned about *"prejudice, its origin and nature, and what could be done in the context of our schools."*

In the 1960s she discovered National Film Board documentaries *"produced or edited by the indigenous or immigrant people talking about their experiences and lives here as minority Canadians."* She spent the rest of her life engaging children and adults in dialogue with the people in these films. When I was in fifth grade, she organized monthly family movie nights in our school gymnasium that had a powerful impact on me. Waves of emotions associated with the film, *"Paddle to the Sea"* still come flooding back to me at unexpected moments.

REPRINTED WITH PERMISSION

During the 1970s Aunty Bette began sharing her approach with students and teachers throughout the school district of North Vancouver, BC where we lived. By 1984, her *Exploring Likenesses and Differences With Film* curriculum had been published by National Film Board and was being enthusiastically received by schools across Canada as a way of reducing prejudice and building esteem about ethnic, disability and lifestyle differences. *"Different viewpoints are encouraged, often debated and, in quite a few situations left open-ended. Basically, we want to gain facts, open closed minds and develop sensitivity to others."* Aunty Bette's book guides children to explore ethnic backgrounds such as Inuit, French Canadian, Polish Canadian, Japanese Canadian and many other cultures. She also has pages that guide children to watch films about a family who live in a lighthouse, a troublesome bully, a boy who is blind and a girl who has spina bifida.

Soon after her book was published, Aunty Bette developed memory problems and eventually found out she had Alzheimer's disease. In response, she helped produce a documentary film so that people could explore, understand and reduce prejudice against people who have Alzheimer's. I feel very fortunate to have had Aunty Bette's guidance as I was growing up.

*ALL QUOTATIONS ARE FROM BETTE HOOD (1984) *EXPLORING LIKENESSES AND DIFFERENCES WITH FILM*. OTTAWA: NATIONAL FILM BOARD OF CANADA. REPRINTED HERE WITH PERMISSION.

Building Inclusive Communities

Every journey begins with a few steps and so getting a few children together to explore diversity is something anyone can try right away. By guiding a few children to relax and have fun as they connect together, we each develop confidence in our abilities to eventually plan expeditions that involve entire communities.

Getting a few children together to explore diversity is something anyone can try right away.

Sandy wasn't having much luck with her efforts to connect with the other kids in her neighborhood. Her preferred method of grabbing someone on the arm, staring at them with her face two inches from theirs and yelling, *"You've got a spider on your head!"* had burnt more than a few bridges. Sandy's mom and Sandy's support worker visited the neighborhood kids one by one, and invited them to come over and play. Most of the children accepted this invitation and were pleasantly surprised to find out how quickly Sandy learned the rules of their favorite games. In turn, Sandy showed them how to play the piano. By playing games and making music together, they all learned new skills for including and being included.

Diversity on the playground

Keep your eyes open for other inclusive travel guides as you explore ways of creating inclusive culture together. Collective inclusive leadership is a powerful tool for social change. Sharing resources helps the possibilities to multiply.

Twenty school staff and twenty students from the sixth grade leadership group had the entire school to ourselves during a workshop about exploring inclusive playground games. During the first hour in the gymnasium, we quickly set competitive mind-sets aside and got totally involved in game after game, but when we went outside to play **Doctor Dodge Ball** (see page 98) two of the students, Trent and Brad, quietly slipped away to play soccer with Merv and Drew, their big brothers who were hanging around outside. They returned as soon as we went back in to the gym, but as soon as we went outside again, they slipped away again, following the lead of the bigger boys to the soccer field. This time we followed too and asked for their help playing **Red Rover Soccer** (see page 55). *"No problem,"* said Merv and Drew. *"Soccer's what we love."* Sure enough, they were incredible soccer players. Talk about touch control and challenge by choice! By the time we stopped for lunch, they were practically signing autographs. We all cheered when they agreed to join us for the rest of the day because all the games seemed just a little more fun with these teenage boys involved. When we drew the day to a close by playing **Mouse Trap** (see page 74), Merv and Drew joined hands with the rest of us and wove in and out of the circle with as much enthusiasm as if they were still wild and innocent five year olds. We had followed these young leaders right into the center of our inclusive circle.

All the games seemed just a little more fun with these teenage boys involved.

Building peace together

Bringing leaders of different groups together can build bridges across prejudice and discrimination. Peer tutoring, leadership training, peer counseling and participatory creative arts are four kinds of cooperative projects that improve relationships between members of different groups. Respectful communication is the key and so games, activities and experiences that teach communication skills work especially well.

We are role models for our younger siblings, cousins, and friends.

Staff at one high school finally decided that they had to do something about years of conflict between the Aboriginal and White students when the violence spread to the girls. We began our search for solutions by forming a partnership between the school and the Aboriginal Health Center. Then, the school counsellor, the First Nations youth worker and I met individually with the young women who had been at the center of the fighting. These troubled young leaders were just as concerned about the violence as we were and a few of the girls had similar ideas for what to do. They wanted the school's annual weekend retreat for peer counsellors to be continued all year. *"Going to that camp in September was great! The Native and Non-native students all got along together. Like, figuring out how to get through that obstacle course sort of forced us to get along together. We really came together and cooperated. Everyone was involved. The talking circle and the drumming were totally cool."* So, we followed the advice of these young elders and set aside one morning per week for an inter-cultural leadership group. Everyone who was invited came and attendance was close to one hundred percent. Cooperative games and group challenges built trust and laughter. Our talking circles and discussions became deeply honest and insightful. The fighting stopped immediately and twelve weeks of meeting together was enough to build a solid peace that lasted for the rest of the school year. Tara and Reene commented that, *"We used to fight because we didn't know each other and no one ever gave us any responsibility to get along. Now we trust each other and we also know that we are role models for our younger siblings, cousins, and friends. We are doing what we are doing for the kids."*

by Harvey Jimmy, age 18

community building in our global village

One or two people can get an entire community involved in cross-cultural exchanges, inter-generational groups, community outreach projects and multicultural festivals. Like throwing a pebble in a pond, the positive ripples continue to spread and have impact long after the event is over.

Shortly after our return to Canada from the Solomon Islands, John and I helped arrange for a group of Solomon Island musicians to come to Canada to perform at the Commonwealth Games. When these two dozen talented young men spent a few days visiting us in our community, they billeted in the homes of various friends who were more than happy to stop listening to our endless South Sea stories long enough to experience the real thing.

Everyone had a fantastic cross-cultural experience, especially our friends with sons. The boys all deserted their computers, television sets and video games in favour of hanging out with their international visitors. They spent so much time riding bicycles, climbing up and down local mountains and playing soccer that there was almost no time to sleep.

One evening after a swim and a picnic by the river, the Solomon Islanders invited the Canadian boys to perform with them. They painted traditional designs on their faces, gave them each an instrument and welcomed them into the band, just as they would have done with the younger boys in their villages on the other side of the Pacific Ocean. For the next few hours, the Canadian kids became more and more in tune with their musical mentors as they watched, listened and learned how to blow bamboo pipes, beat drums with a thong, and shake rattles so big they had to be held in two hands. They performed on and on without missing a beat while the Canadian adults joined with the girls and small boys and danced around and around the pan-pipers in a circle of joy and laughter.

Like throwing a pebble in a pond, the positive ripples continue to spread and have impact long after the event is over.

FROM **LINK MAGAZINE** (1992). HONIARA: SOLOMON ISLANDS DEVELOPMENT TRUST. REPRINTED WITH PERMISSION.

We Made A Difference Today

When I look out at the stars, I smile…

Garth was really funny and made us laugh.

We went to the forest museum. It was easy to get my wheelchair on the train but I thought the look-out tower would be impossible until everyone helped carry me up. It was cool!

We made up songs about each person's name in every different language.

Ariana drew pictures of what we were singing about.

The big kids were way nicer than they usually are.

We played this really neat hide and seek game. I sat so still that I found a frog, and a great blue heron too, then a butterfly landed right on me.

I held the feather in the talking circle.

We learned that worms are Deaf just like me. Birds can hear. Trees use Sign Language. Clouds are pictures so I think they are Deaf too.

Mara and I got along better than we used to.

I'm not playing by myself so much anymore, but I'm asking other people and letting people join in.

I made some friends and I'm not so shy anymore.

We folded cranes. When we make 1000 the wars will all end.

I didn't want today to end, it's still too early for me to learn to get along all by myself.

Yay! I'm going back again tomorrow.

Tatatatami

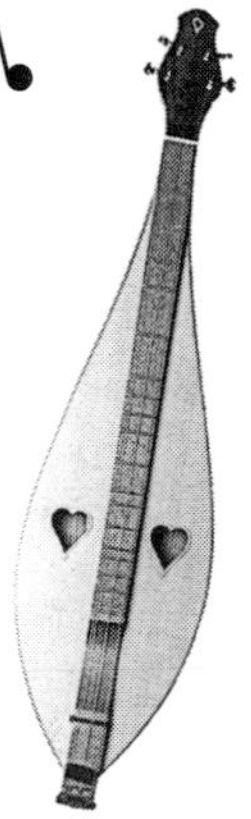

Well the sun comes up
and it goes back down
but guess what
it comes back up
now I don't know about this round and round
but I like to think the sun can't get enough
and you see that's like me, I'm a little like that light
and when we sing I feel we're shining on
so if this is a goodbye, I hope our little song will carry on.

Well the tree grows up
and it falls back down
the seed in the ground grows up
well I don't know about this up and down
but I like to think the tree can't get enough
and the tree is like me, I shake like a leaf
but when we sing I stand so tall and strong
so if this is a goodbye I hope our little song will carry on.

People grow up
and they fall back down
in between they try a lot of stuff
I don't know if they win or they lose
but I do not think these people sing enough
so agree with me, I'm not always right
but when we sing I feel so safe and warm
so, if this is a goodbye, I hope our little song will carry on.

I hope our little song will carry on.

LYRICS TO "TATATATAMI" BY RICK SCOTT,
FROM HIS ALBUM *RICK AROUND THE ROCK* ©1992 GRAND POOBAH MUSIC.
REPRINTED HERE WITH PERMISSION.

"It's delightful when your imaginations come true, isn't it?"

ANNE SHIRLEY
— FROM L. M. MONTGOMERY (1908) **ANNE OF GREEN GABLES**

Part 4:

More Resources for Exploring Diversity

A Few Resourceful Organizations

American Camping Association, 5000 State Road 67 North, Martinsville, IN 46151-7902
Telephone: (765) 342-8456 • Website: www.acacamps.org

A community of camp professionals dedicated to enriching the lives of children and adults through the camp experience.

Canadian Camping Association, Box 74030, Edmonton, Alberta T5K 2S7
Toll Free Telephone: (877) 427-6958 • Website: www.kidscamps.com/canadian-camping

A non-profit federation of provincial camping associations, promoting organzied camping for all populations throughout Canada. Ontario Camping Association also provides leadership to Canadian organizations who support organized camping. For information about conferences, workshops and training sessions offered by OCA contact:

Ontario Camping Association, 250 Merton St., Suite 403, Toronto, Ontario M4S 1B1
Telephone: (416) 485-0425 • Website: www.ontcamp.on.ca

Children's Music Network, Box 1341, Evanston, IL 60204-1341
Telephone: (847) 733-8003 • Website: www.cmnonline.org

Members recognize children's music as a powerful means of encouraging cooperation, celebrating diversity, building self-esteem, promoting respect and responsibility for our environment and cultivating an understanding of nonviolence and social justice.

Inclusion Press International, 24 Thome Crescent, Toronto, Ontario M6H 2S5
Telephone: (416) 658-5363 • Fax: (416) 658-5067 • Website: www.inclusion.com

Inclusion Press, developed by Jack Pearpoint and Marsha Forest, strives to produce readable, accessible, user-friendly books and resources about full inclusion in school, work and community of children and adults who have disabilities. Marsha died in 2000 but her spirit continues to guide people around the world.

National Film Board of Canada, Box 6100, Station Centre-ville, Montreal, Quebec H3C 3H5
Toll Free Telephone: (800) 267-7710 • Website: www.nfb.ca

Created in 1939, the National Film Board of Canada (NFB) is a public agency that produces and distributes films and other audio-visual works which reflect Canada to Canadians and the rest of the world. The focus is on appreciation and understanding of multi-culturalism and diversity.

New Society Publishers, P.O. Box 189, Gabriola Island, British Columbia V0R 1X0
Telephone: (250) 247-9737 • Fax: (250) 247-7471 • Book Orders: 1-800-567-6772
Website: www.newsociety.com

NSP's mission is to publish books that contribute in fundamental ways to building an ecologically sustainable and just society, and to do so with the least possible impact upon the environment, in a manner that models that vision. Their catalog includes a growing number of books for educators and parents.

People For Peace Website: www.people4peace.com

"Every act of compassion makes a difference and every day counts for a better world; one heart, one day at a time."

This global network aims to link individuals and organizations with resources and information for co-creating a better world. So far over 14,000 organizations and thousands more individuals are keeping in touch through this website.

Project Adventure, Box 100, Hamilton, MA 01936
Telephone: (978) 468-7981 • Website: www.pa.org

Adventure education is learning that incorporates all the elements of an adventure: surprise, stimulation, support and significance. Children and adults challenge themselves to go beyond perceived boundaries, to think in new ways and to work with others to solve problems.

Project Nature Connect, Box 1605, Friday Harbor, WA 98250
Telephone: (360) 378-6313 • Website: www.ecopsych.com

Director, Michael J. Cohen has books, internet courses and workshops showing how to walk nature's path to wellness for people and the planet. Although Dr. Cohen's courses are for adults, many of Dr. Cohen's students follow his processes while guiding children to connect with nature.

Simulation Training Systems, Box 910, Del Mar, CA 92014
Toll Free Telephone: (800) 942-2900 • Website: www.stsintl.com

Producers of many cross-cultural simulation games, including the classic experiential cross-cultural communication game, BaFá BaFá. In only two hours participants become members of one culture, visit another culture and examine the impact of cross-cultural contact. There is also a junior version especially designed for young children.

A Few Books

Blood-Patterson, Peter (1988) *Rise Up Singing: 1200 songs, words, chords, sources.* Bethlehem, PA: Sing Out Corporation.

Bodine, Richard et al. (1994) *Creating The Peaceable School: A comprehensive program for teaching conflict resolution.* Champaign, IL: Research Press.

Caduto, Michael and Bruchac, Joseph (1994) *Keepers Of Life: Discovering plants through native stories and earth activities for children.* Calgary, AB: Fifth House Publishers.

Cornell, Joseph (1989) *Sharing The Joy Of Nature: Nature activities for all ages.* Nevada City, CA: Dawn Publications.

Cartledge, Gwendolyn (1996) *Cultural Diversity And Social Skills Instruction: Understanding ethnic and gender differences.* Champaign, IL: Research Press.

Gibbs, Jeanne (1995) *Tribes: A new way of learning and being together.* Santa Rosa, CA: CenterSource Systems.

Goldstein, Arnold (1988, revised in 1999) *The Prepare Curriculum: Teaching prosocial competencies.* Champaign, IL: Research Press.

Golick, Margie (1981) *Deal Me In!: The use of playing cards in teaching and learning.* New York, NY: Jeffrey Norton Publishers.

Golick, Margie (1986) *Reading, Writing And Rummy: More than 100 card games to develop language, social skills, number concepts and problem solving strategies.* Markham, ON: Pembroke Publishers.

Greenstein, Doreen et al. (1997) *Backyards And Butterflies: Ways to include children with disabilities in outdoor activities.* Cambridge, MA: Brookline Books.

Havens, Mark (1992) *Bridges to Accessibility.* Hamilton, MA: Project Adventure.

Henley, Thom. (1989, revised 1996). *Rediscovery: Ancient pathways new directions, outdoor activities based on native traditions.* Vancouver, BC: Lone Pine Publishing.

Hill, Linda (1998) *Discovering Connections: A guide to the fun of bridging disability differences.* Duncan, BC: Building Bridges Consulting.

Jackson, Nancy et al. (1983) *Getting Along With Others: Teaching social effectiveness to children.* Champaign, IL: Research Press.

Khalsa, Siri Nam (1996) *Group Exercises For Enhancing Social Skills And Self-esteem.* Sarasota, FL: Professional Resource Press.

Levin, Diane (1994) *Teaching Young Children In Violent Times: Building a peaceable classroom.* Gabriola Island, BC: New Society Publishers.

Luvmour, Sambhava and Josette (1990) *Everyone Wins!: Cooperative games and activities.* Gabriola Island, BC: New Society Publishers.

MacLeod, Elizabeth (1990) *The Games Book From The Editors Of OWL Magazine.* Markham, ON: Greey de Pencier Books.

Merritt, Rob and Walley, Donald (1977) *The Group Leader's Handbook: Resources, techniques and survival skills.* Champaign, IL: Research Press.

Orlick, Terry (1978, republished in 1995) *The Cooperative Sports And Games Book.* New York, NY: Pantheon Books.

Orlick, Terry (1982, republished in 1995) *The Second Cooperative Sports And Games Book.* New York, NY: Pantheon Books.

Prutzman, Priscilla et al. (1988) *The Friendly Classroom For A Small Planet: A handbook on creative approaches to living and problem solving for children.* Gabriola Island, BC: New Society Publishers.

Rohnke, Karl (1988) *The Bottomless Bag.* Cambridge, MA: Project Adventure.

Sapon-Shevin, Mara. (1999) *Because We Can Change the World: A Practical Guide to Building Cooperative Inclusive Classroom Communities.* Needham Heights, MA: Allyn and Bacon.

Smith, Charles (1993) *The Peaceful Classroom: 162 easy activities to teach preschoolers compassion and cooperation.* Beltsville, MD: Gryphon House.

Sobel, Jeffrey (1983) *Everybody Wins: Non-competitive play for young children.* New York, NY: Walker and Company.

Walker, Hill et al. (1983) *The Walker Social Skills Curriculum: The Accepts Program.* Austin, TX: Pro Ed Resources.

Building bridges between our divisions
I reach out to you.
Will you reach out to me?
With all of our voices and all of our visions
Friends, we could make such sweet harmony.

COMPOSED BY THE WOMEN OF THE PEACE CAMP ON GREENHAM COMMON, ENGLAND IN 1983.

Part 5:

Behind the Scenes:
The contributors to this Book

About the Author - Linda Hill

Linda Hill, PhD, is a psychologist, educator and child care worker. She has held an adjunct appointment as assistant professor in the psychology department at the University of Victoria, Victoria, British Columbia since 1998. She combines learnings from the fields of cross-cultural communication, social learning and participatory education to help groups and organizations bring diverse people together to build bridges across differences. Linda enjoys visiting communities through her workshops, participatory research projects and books. Her travels have taken her from high-rise buildings in large cities to leaf houses in small villages and every place in between including recreation centers, camps, schools, hospitals, government departments, community agencies, neighborhoods and families.

Linda works in partnership with many different groups and organizations on Vancouver Island. She has also worked in communities across Canada as well as England, Kiribati, United States, Federated States of Micronesia (where she and her life-partner, John, taught in 1987) and the Solomon Islands (where they worked from 1991 to 1993 as CUSO cooperants).

Linda and John developed Building Bridges Consulting to share their vision of an interconnected world where the gifts within every living being are acknowledged, valued and supported to grow. They have each spent most of their lives learning how to share the right and the responsibility we all have to care for each other and for our Earth. Many of their explorations into diversity have been within the Cowichan Valley on Vancouver Island where they spend as much time as possible messing about in small boats in the Salish Sea and contributing to local community organizations such as the Cowichan Valley Naturalist Society, the Cowichan Community Land Trust, and the Cowichan Valley Intercultural and Immigrant Aid Society.

John and Linda

Connecting Kids is Linda's second major publication.
Her 1998 book *Discovering Connections* is being shared by diverse people around the world and is being discovered by teachers and students in high schools, colleges and universities who are exploring inclusion, diversity and fun.

She can be reached at:

✯✯✯✯ Building Bridges Consulting

P.O. Box 156, Duncan, BC, Canada V9L 3X3
Phone or Fax : 1-250-746-1529 or
in Canada and USA phone or fax toll free: 1-888-746-1529
TTY: 1-250-746-1539
E-mail: bridges@island.net
Visit the web page at: www.island.net/~bridges/

About the Entertainer - Rick Scott

Rick Scott combines music and humour in songs for all ages. He has released four award winning children's recordings and performed over a thousand concerts around the globe. His warm-hearted keynote performances enliven gatherings of caregivers and educators. Rick is a spokesperson for the Down Syndrome Research Foundation in Vancouver. He wrote the song "Angels Do" for his granddaughter who stars with him in a music video celebrating children who have special needs.

Discography:

- **Making Faces** (2000) cassette and CD
- **Angels Do** (1998) VHS Video
- **Philharmonic Fool** (1995) cassette and CD
- **Rick Around the Rock** (1992) cassette only
- **The Electric Snowshoe** (1989) cassette only
- **Pied Pear Elementary** (1985) cassette only

Contact Rick c/o:

Great Scott! Productions

#408 – 336 East First Avenue, Vancouver, BC, Canada V5T 1A9
Phone (604) 736-7676 • Fax (604) 739-0936
Email: rickscot@smartt.com • Website: www.rick-scott.com

Connecting with Rick:

In 1998 I attended one of Rick's entertaining and inspiring keynote performances for adults who work with children. His music and stories completely resonated with my own enthusiasm for the adventures of exploring diversity. Later that morning I got into a conversation with Valley Hennell (Rick's manager, collaborator, and life partner) and immediately felt a similar connection. A year later, I got up my courage and asked them to write the foreword to *Connecting Kids*. I am still amazed that two such busy people would take the time to read an early draft of the book, find the value and the fun in what was still a very ponderous document, and then spend an entire day with me and several hours of follow-up getting the words to the foreword just right. On top of all this, they permitted me to reprint three of Rick's songs. Thank you Rick and Valley for all your generosity!

LINDA HILL

About the Artists

Ian Finlayson studied at Sheridan College in Oakville, Ontario, and has worked as a professional illustrator and designer within the graphics arts industry for more than fifteen years. Ian illustrated Linda's first book *Discovering Connections*. For *Connecting Kids* he created four more watercolor paintings of hands connecting through play for the front cover. He also worked with Linda's photographs to create a series of pencil sketches of children at play that are found within the book. Ian lives with his family in Cobble Hill, BC, Canada. *He can be reached by email at finlyson@islandnet.com*

Robert McKenzie has worked in the graphic arts field since 1984 and has operated his own studio in Duncan, BC, Canada since 1992. Robert works on a variety of projects including commercial graphics for business, arts and events promotion. Although he has been involved in computers since the beginning of the digital revolution, Robert values the importance of working with pencil and paper. He drew the cartoons for this project by hand and then made minor revisions on the computer. *Robert can be reached by phone at (250) 746-4811 or e-mail: mcrob@island.net*

Ethan Dunham is a professional graphic designer and illustrator based in Wilmington, Delaware, USA. He also runs a small internet font foundry called Fonthead Design. For this book, Ethan created the animal drawings accompanying the text and designed several of the typefaces.

To view more of these fonts and drawings, visit his web site at http://www.fonthead.com

Danika Carlson, age 8, writes, "My Mom was born in the Philippines, my Dad was born in Canada and I was born in Canada. I like playing in my make-believe art studio that I built in my Dad's carport. To draw, I think of pictures in my mind and then I copy them. One photo shows how I dressed up as Cleopatra on Halloween when I was six years old and the other was taken this year at the Crystal Gardens in Victoria, BC." Danika contributed four drawings on pages 4, 24, 46 and 126.
She can be reached by e-mail through Building Bridges at bridges@island.net

Jana Vance, age 13, writes, "I was born in Thailand and came to Canada at the age of four. I learned to draw by watching animated Walt Disney movies. I draw from my emotions. I draw based on how I feel during the day. When I think about differences I think that I don't care what color people are. I like everyone. One photo shows me with my Thai doll when I was six years old. The other was taken this year at school." Jana contributed four cartoons on pages 4, 6, 8 and 10.
She can be reached by e-mail at j&avance@telus.net

Harvey Jimmy, age 18, is a volunteer youth leader and a self-taught artist who enjoys both drawing and carving. "I began drawing in pre-school. At first all my pictures were of eagles and whales. Then, I began copying the works of other Native artists that I found in books at school. Eventually, I developed my own style. I thought it would be cool if Linda's book had some Native art in it." He contributed two drawings on pages 10 and 150.
Harvey can be reached at: gr8_one17@hotmail.com

Cowichan Valley Intercultural and Immigrant Aid Society (CVIIAS) is a non-profit society with a mission to build mutual respect, trust, support and education in the culturally diverse community of Cowichan Valley. CVIIAS offers many educational, employment, and support services to refugees and other new immigrants. Every year CVIIAS sponsors several community educational events such as a Camp Rainbow: A multicultural summer camp and the International Children's Art Festival held in 1985. CVIIAS contributed art from that festival by the following young artists:

The following individuals also contributed stories, art and creative writing:

I also wish to acknowledge "Don," "Ken," "Jade," "Rosemarie," and many other individuals whose stories are told on other pages, but whose names have been changed to protect their privacy. Thank you to each of you for what you taught me by sharing these experiences with me.

Photo credits:

About the Designer – Kim Barnard

Kim Barnard is a home-based graphic designer who operates her freelance business, Graphic Details, in the picturesque surroundings of Shawnigan Lake, BC. With over ten years experience in trade shops from Vancouver to Victoria, she is pleased to bring her skills to bear in helping communicate the thoughts and ideas contained in this book. She offers a full-service approach, with copywriting assistance, prepress coordination and print-buying consultation services for her clients. Kim is an Adobe Certified Expert in Photoshop 5.0 and teaches a computer graphics class at a private boarding school nearby. She reads countless manuals, "just for fun," to aim to master the technology so that she is free to explore the possibilities. With projects such as this, she strives to bring all of the text and graphic elements together to leave an unforgettable impression on the reader. "More than words on paper," she explains, "is what you will find within." *Kim can be reached by e-mail at kimba_rnard@hotmail.com*

Designer's Notes on the Making of the Book:

I love my work as a graphic designer, and it is always a privilege to work with material such as this. When Linda first showed me the *Connecting Kids* project, I felt a trembling sense of awe at the far-reaching potential of the message she had to share. The stories touched me deeply and rekindled memories of my own childhood and school experiences. There was no doubt in my mind how different things might have been had we all learned practical ways to show love and support to one another during those often tumultuous growing up years. As a parent now of two preschool-age children, I am more motivated than ever to "help make the world a better place" by teaching my kids to be leaders who can share the joy in life and make a difference. This book is an invaluable guide to building awareness and learning those skills.

What made this project even more special was that Linda was at a stage with the writing of *Connecting Kids* where she welcomed all kinds of input and suggestions. It certainly was a wonderful opportunity to be asked to contribute on that level as well. I want to thank her for allowing me the freedom to really practice my craft, for having the enthusiasm that made it easy for me to delight in the material, for being so receptive to trying new things, for having the vision and perseverance to see this project through to its ultimate form, and for possessing the courage not to settle for economy over quality. She truly loves her work and it shows. I wish her every success with her desire to reach people with her message and make a difference.

I also must thank Ethan Dunham for providing some pivotal inspiration in the form of his delightfully whimsical fonts and critters. It all started with a chance visit to his Fonthead Design website. Despite being across the continent and several time zones, Ethan dropped everything and rose to the challenge of creating, in record time, a custom set of animal critters to adorn our sidebar text. His work just seemed made for this piece. And, if I might add, the Fonthead Design T-shirt is simply a "must have"!

I gratefully acknowledge the support of my husband and best friend Cameron who, along with providing in-house technical support, was my understanding and supportive cheering section. He gamely went without hot-cooked meals, bag lunches or ironed shirts (among other things) while this project was in progress! I also have many other family members and friends whom I hope to "reconnect" with — by presenting them with a copy of the finished book, of course — now that the work's all done and it's time to play!

Lastly, thank you to Steve Fisher, who first introduced me to Linda, and began the start of what is now (and still is, after two books!) a beautiful friendship.

Acknowledgments

In this book that goes right back to the roots of my childhood, I have many, many people to thank. I couldn't have put this book together without you.

❀ My parents **Diana** and **Ted Hill**; grandparents **Audrey** and **Ronald Jackson**; siblings **Guida**, **Ted**, **Wilda**, **Michael**, and **Randy**; everyone in my extended families of **Allardices**, **Eatons**, **Fees**, **Halls**, **Jacksons**, **Jacobsens** and **Sculls**. My life-partner and soulmate **John Scull**; my step-children **Kathy** and **Charley**; my nieces and nephews **Ted**, **Jan**, **Jesse**, **Jennifer**, **Ben**, **Westley**, **Deanna**, **Tosh** and **Sam**. Thank you all for helping to make my childhood and adulthood adventurously happy.

❀ **Mr. James Inkster** who founded Carson Graham Secondary School in North Vancouver, BC with a vision of an inclusive cross-cultural learning environment for students of all cultures, abilities, talents and interests.

❀ North Vancouver Outdoor School, Pender Street YWCA, Victoria YM-YWCA, Island Deaf and Hard of Hearing Center, Staff and children in Summer Adventure Day Camp for providing me with so many opportunities to explore diversity and develop my inclusive leadership skills.

❀ Students and instructors at University of British Columbia, University of Victoria, and the Community College of Micronesia for guiding me to integrate research with practice.

❀ Deaf and Hard of Hearing children, their families and their friends in the Victoria area, especially the **Golinskys**, **Andersons**, **Dunns**, **Bells**, **Gordons**, **Walcots**, **Anne Young**, **Lana Ruddick**, **Gloria (Wheeldon) Dumont**, and **Bobby Joe Wheeldon**. Bobby Joe built so many bridges of friendship and understanding before she left the world too soon and too suddenly in 1991.

❀ The children and their families and my colleagues who supported my work, learning and play in schools, hospitals, health centers and community settings during the 1970s, '80s, and '90s. I would especially like to honour **Mr. Chuck Curtis**, **Dr. Bill Gaddes**, and **Dr. John Scull** who taught all of us involved with children at Cedar Lodge Center during the 1970s to build on children's strengths.

❀ Our friends and colleagues in Micronesia and the Solomon Islands who welcomed us into their South Pacific communities and gave us gifts of time and laughter, especially **Kardas Nena** and her niece **Erika** on Pohnpei, and all the families in our Guadalcanal neighborhoods of Naha and Gilbert Camp.

❀ Everyone who joined in on journeys into our communities over the years of developing and writing my first book *Discovering Connections*, especially members of the Cowichan Valley Independent Living Resource Center.

(continued on the next page)

(Acknowledgments continued)

❀ The groups and organizations who sponsored the *Connecting Kids* Workshops and the individuals who participated and gave me the feedback I needed to make *Connecting Kids* practical and educational: Bulkley Valley Supported Child Care Services; Cowichan Community Centre, Cowichan Valley (CV) Association for Community Living, CV Early Childhood Educators, CV Family Support Program, CV Intercultural and Immigrant Aid Society, CV Naturalist Society, CV Supported Child Care, Frances Kelsey Secondary School, Growing Together Young Parent Program, Hiiye'yu Lelum (House of Friendship) Society, Koksilah Elementary School, Nanaimo Child Development Centre, Malaspina University-College Native Indian Teacher Education Program, Ontario Camping Association, Victoria Association for Community Living, the Victoria Ups and Downs Family Support Group, and the following Cowichan Tribes Programs: Education and Culture, Lalum'utul'Smun'eem Child and Family Services, Youth Crime Prevention Team, TseWulTun Health Centre.

❀ Many individuals have given feedback about the various drafts of *Connecting Kids*. I would especially like to thank **Charlene Antinuk, Cathy Bone, Judi Bailey, Zerena Caplin, Tammy Gilmour, Sarah Mathison, Judith McDowell, Chris Plant, Diane Salo, Reva Schafer, John Scull, Genevieve Singleton, Robin Thomas** and **Val Townsend.**

In designing *Connecting Kids* I have had the good fortune to collaborate with **Kim Barnard** once again. As she did with *Discovering Connections*, Kim has applied her extraordinary graphic design gifts to transform my words and ideas into a work of art. We have both enjoyed everyone's stories and art, and the creative energies of professional illustrators **Ian Finlayson, Robert McKenzie** and **Ethan Dunham.**

And, to repeat my words from the beginning of the book, I honour everyone who has ever participated in inventing, reinventing and sharing so many wonderful games, activities and experiences. Thank you for joining in life's never-ending relay of joy, love and laughter by passing your ideas on to me so that I can pass them on to others.

Linda D. Hill

Linda D. Hill, Ph.D.
Registered Psychologist

Index of Games, Activities and Experiences

(Index continued)

(Index continued)

(Index continued)

(Index continued)

More Games, Activities and Experiences in Nature...

Connecting Skill: _____

Title: _____

Equipment and Supplies: _____

Description: _____

_____

_____

_____

_____

Connecting Skill: _____

Title: _____

Equipment and Supplies: _____

Description: _____

_____

_____

_____

_____

Use this space
for inventing new
possibilities!

Connecting Skill: _____

Title: _____

Equipment and Supplies: _____

Description: _____

_____

_____

_____

_____

Connecting Skill: _____

Title: _____

Equipment and Supplies: _____

Description: _____

_____

_____

_____

_____

Connecting Skill: _____

Title: _____

Equipment and Supplies: _____

Description: _____

_____

_____

_____

_____

Record your own
recipes for
exploring diversity
together.

Connecting Skill: _____

Title: _____

Equipment and Supplies: _____

Description: _____

_____

_____

_____

_____

More Games, Activities and Experiences in Nature...

Connecting Skill: _____

Title: _____

Equipment and Supplies: _____

Description: _____

_____

_____

_____

_____

Challenge yourself to think up more imaginative adventures.

Connecting Skill: _____

Title: _____

Equipment and Supplies: _____

Description: _____

_____

_____

_____

_____

Connecting Skill: _____

Title: _____

Equipment and Supplies: _____

Description: _____

_____

_____

_____